ANSWERING CH

Answering
Chief Seattle

Albert Furtwangler

A Samuel & Althea Stroum Book

UNIVERSITY OF WASHINGTON PRESS
SEATTLE AND LONDON

Library of Congress Cataloging-in-Publication Data
Furtwangler, Albert, 1942–
Answering Chief Seattle / Albert Furtwangler.
p. cm.
"A Samuel and Althea Stroum book."
Includes bibliographical references.
ISBN 0–295–97633–0 (alk. paper)
1. Seattle, Chief, 1790–1866 — Oratory. 2. Speeches, addresses, etc., Suquamish. 3. Suquamish Indians — History. 4. Puget Sound Region (Wash.) — History. 5. Human ecology. I. Seattle, Chief, 1790–1866. II. Title.
E99.S85S433 1997
979.7'004979 — dc21
[B]   97-8896
                              CIP

The paper used in this publication meets the minimum requirements of American National Standard for Information Sciences–Permanence of Paper for Printed Library Materials, ANSI Z39.48-1984.

This book is published with the assistance of a grant from the Stroum Book Fund, established through the generosity of Samuel and Althea Stroum.

CONTENTS

PREFACE

THE CHAPTERS THAT FOLLOW attempt to probe, weigh, stretch, and reconsider a literary and historical puzzle. In 1887 a columnist in a Seattle newspaper published a long speech by the Indian leader after whom the city was named. The writer claimed that Seattle (or Sealth) had made this speech at a great meeting on the waterfront in the 1850s, a good thirty years earlier. The speech was a reply to some remarks by the first territorial governor, Isaac I. Stevens, and it protested against the disappearance of Indian lands and ways under the pressure of recent white settlement. Over the years this speech has been modified, rewritten, embellished, broadcast, excerpted, popularized, discussed, and carved into many a monument. But what exactly it is, how it emerged into print, and what its occasion was or could have been have remained inadequately explained.

No other source or record of this speech has turned up since 1887. No earlier notes, fragments, or closely parallel speeches by Seattle have come to light. What has emerged instead over the decades is a heightened awareness about Indian oratory, a recognition that it has often been celebrated by literate Europeans and Americans for their own purposes. It has been used to hold Indians at a distance, as noble, tragic, but very different peoples. Speeches of protest, in particular, show up again and again in American history as documents that prove the greatness of a "vanished" or "vanishing" race.

Is the Seattle speech a surviving record of an actual event? Or is it a fabrication from white men's pens and presses, a subtle reshaping of history designed to mold Indian ideas or characters into a justification of modern developments? The available evidence lends itself to both interpretations. The text printed in 1887 contains many telltale touches that seem not contrived but authentic, accurate reflections of conditions and Indian beliefs in the 1850s. On the other hand, it is also a manifestly translated text. It bears many marks of the white American settler who wrote it and of the like-minded readers he addressed.

To see into this puzzle, this book sifts textual, historical, and literary evidence. The opening chapters look, in turn, at the legendary dimensions of the speech as it is usually presented (as a Great Confrontation between a towering Indian and a short and officious American empire builder); at the textual problems plaguing every version of the speech since 1887; and at the historical circumstances of every known meeting between Seattle and Governor Stevens in the early 1850s. These chapters explicate the speech as we have it and explore most of its puzzles in full detail.

But to press further, the remaining chapters pursue another tactic by turning to voices that answer this speech, whatever its source may be. The central question of Seattle's speech is the relation of a people to the land, and in this respect the speech closely resembles other American texts of its time. Famous passages by Thomas Jefferson, Walt Whitman, and Nathaniel Hawthorne constitute three typical American answers to Chief Seattle, even though these writers never heard or read any of his words. The ideas in these writings also appear in the words and deeds of someone who certainly did. Governor Stevens has left substantial records about his own relations with Indians, to the West, and to the exploration and settlement of America. They do not directly show any trace of a Great Confrontation on the Seattle waterfront. But they reveal a larger encounter between Stevens's comprehensive intelligence and the pleas that inform the Seattle speech. They unfold a long-term clash and accommodation between the ambitions of a mid-century, eastern-American patriot and the needs of the displaced, indigenous people of the Far West.

The book closes by attempting to measure the speech against two further backgrounds: the geography and monuments to Indians that still stand out around the modern city of Seattle, and the range of oral literature that survives as a heritage of Northwest Indians. The Seattle speech did not conclude Indian history, as some of its lines suggest. It has also been answered and illuminated by persisting physical landmarks and by persisting, complex tales and reminiscences.

The aim of this study is not to authenticate or debunk the speech, but to bring to light the many layers of its mystery – inadequate evidence about its origins, conflicting evidence about its main ideas, and conflicting attitudes toward those ideas in the American tradition. The speech printed in 1887, authentic or not, seems likely to endure as a provocative challenge to any thoughtful reader of later times. The question at issue is how Americans here and now can develop an honest claim or feeling for a place in the Far West. Jefferson, Whitman, Hawthorne, Seattle, Stevens, and others we will meet all provide thoughtful but partial and very different answers.

One final note about my own stake in this debate. By birth I am myself a Seattleite, the son of a father born along the shores of the Duwamish River in 1908, the grandson of a German immigrant who stepped off a transcontinental train around 1889. With ancestors now buried in its soil; with a childhood spent in its schools, on its streets, and in open boats around Puget Sound; with cousins and children of cousins now long settled around its shores; with schoolmates established in lives and businesses over all its hills, I am part of Seattle and always will be. I and mine have been there for a century and more. Yet by training and experience

I have also sunk roots far away: in academic libraries in the eastern states and in Canada; in classrooms and family life in New York, New Jersey, and New England; in German lessons to connect (however faintly) with forebears in Freiburg-im-Breisgau. For many years I have traveled back often to Oregon and Washington; over the past fifteen years I have worked on a series of books about the possibilities of life in America as a continental nation.

These strains in my own sense of place may account for some strains in this study. The imagery of Seattle's country has been vivid before me as I have scribbled in a room lined with books. On the other hand, exact phrases from Alexander Hamilton and James Madison have sometimes echoed in my ears as I have walked the West Seattle neighborhood or ridden a ferry across Elliott Bay. Much of this book was composed in snowbound Sackville, New Brunswick; much of it has been revised and reorganized during weeks at the Oregon Coast, at a spot where Indian stories tell of ancient voyages across the sea to a land of tall bamboo. As a result of such reflections across a continent, passages from Whitman and Hawthorne have crystalized moods in my own identity. At times, returning to scenes transformed beyond recognition, I have felt the deep urgency of Seattle's protests. At times, I have been surprised by the breadth and depth of what Stevens managed to discern in a very short life. At other times, I have been appalled that he and his contemporaries came so close and yet missed so much.

With this background it has proved impossible for me to neatly resolve the puzzles of the famous speech. I have had to weigh and respect not just one voice, but many voices out of the American past; they have echoed not at a distance but deep within.

My work on this book has been fostered directly by institutions on both Atlantic and Pacific shores. Mount Allison University has provided grants from the Crake Foundation and other research funds. I have received friendly help at the libraries of Harvard, Yale, the University of Washington, and the National Archives–Pacific Northwest Region. For special courtesies I must thank Vince Keuter of the Washington State Library, Glenda Pearson of Newspapers and Microforms at the University of Washington library, Carolyn J. Marr of the Seattle Museum of History and Industry, and Anne Ward of the R. P. Bell Library at Mount Allison.

David M. Buerge and Rudolph Kaiser have answered questions very directly by mail. Robert Hunt, a fellow researcher on Lewis and Clark, has sent me recent clippings from Seattle.

Three anonymous readers for the University of Washington Press have provided searching and well-informed suggestions, which I have adopted or at least considered carefully, to improve this work. An invitation to lecture on this subject at Washington State University/Vancouver afforded timely incentives for revising a central chapter and reconsidering its structure; Tim Hunt of the wsu English Department co-ordinated that visit and lecture.

Cathy Colwell transferred several versions of my manuscript onto word processing equipment swiftly and cheerfully.

My parents, other family members, and early teachers in Seattle have imparted their varied experiences in developing rootedness there. My wife has shared years of experience in dwelling and returning across many borders. Together, she and I have often had to give Donne's words fresh meaning: to make "one little room an everywhere."

THE SPEECH AND ITS SETTING

CHAPTER 1

The Legendary Tableau

CHIEF SEATTLE has become world famous in this century for a long and moving speech he made in the 1850s, just before his lands were taken from him and his people. According to a printed account that appeared many years later, Governor Isaac A. Stevens spoke first, outlining the general terms of a proposed treaty. Then Seattle towered over the little governor and spoke extensively, seeing prophetically into the future of his region and even into the global dilemmas in which we now live. A young doctor, Henry A. Smith, took notes as the speech was being translated on the spot; it was his version that appeared in the late 1880s. Since then, the speech has circulated more widely in official and popular histories of the city of Seattle and its region. More recently, it has been reprinted and widely broadcast as a challenging admonition against modern industrialization, pollution, imperialism, and civilized folly. In various versions its language has been quoted, excerpted, and repeated in speeches, broadcasts, films, pamphlets, and children's books. It has become known worldwide as a treasure of indigenous American wisdom.

Again and again the speech has been presented as a symbolic encounter between indigenous America, represented by Chief Seattle, and industrialized or imperialist America, represented by Governor Stevens. The speech has seemed to record the voice of an Indian of the far wilderness protesting against the claims of westward-marching power and usurpation. It seems to pit truth against injustice and wisdom against willful blindness, and to resonate through the decades with ever-more-evident depths of

3

prophetic accuracy. It also seems to promise that ancient ways will persist and prevail despite the temporary and illusory victories of nineteenth-century invasion and development.

Many readers are aware that the drama of the speech has been heightened and amplified in recent years. Encounters of the 1850s and printed records of the 1880s and 1890s have been altered to fit modern circumstances. In 1987, a German scholar named Rudolph Kaiser was able to trace several versions of the speech that lay behind its great modern vogue in Europe and around the world. He presented four different, loosely related versions: Smith's original publication, which first appeared in 1887; a 1969 translation made by William Arrowsmith, from Smith's "Victorian" language into modern English; a new speech, based on Arrowsmith's, but freely composed by Ted Perry in 1970–71 for an ecological filmscript; and an adaptation of Perry's speech, made into an inscription at the Spokane World's Fair in 1974. Out of these sources, the speech had become a token of the modern ecology movement.

Later articles have revealed that even Kaiser's carefully printed versions are not quite accurate or complete. In 1989 Ted Perry reprinted his own version of the speech, with a brief explanation of how it was taken over and revised for a television film. Around the same time an extensive review of the whole problem was undertaken for a documentary radio broadcast in California. The resulting script, by Daniel J. Miller and Patricia R. Miller, includes an annotated bibliography of eighty-six items. This study brings out a complicated history of textual transmission, with subtle and puzzling variations between the time of Smith's first publication in 1887 and the widespread Arrowsmith-Perry-television versions of the 1970s.

Furthermore, some perplexing questions haunt the seemingly

"authentic" version, too — the one published in 1887 by Henry A. Smith, based on his records and recollections. No manuscripts or notes of this speech have ever come to light. No witnesses or records corroborate his account. Smith directly states that his version is an imperfect rendering of a speech he heard through translation, some thirty-three years or more before he put it into print. What any current reader can study therefore is at best an echo of Chief Seattle's words and ideas, or, at worst, an account woven from faulty memory, imperfect notes, or pure fabulation.

Nevertheless, the legend of Seattle and his speech remains irrepressible. It appears in dozens of publications, including widely respected histories, collections of American documents, and anthologies of American literature. To be sure, many recent anthologies have deleted it or reprinted it with notes of caution, but to the historian it still presents an intriguing example of how a story or an idea can persist in the face of overwhelming evidence that should demolish it. To the student of literature it presents a no less sobering instance of the exalting and dissemination of a very suspicious text. And in modern America the importance of this legend is yet wider and deeper. It continues to dramatize two radically different understandings of American origins and values.

This conflict of values has framed the speech not just recently but for many decades. Here, for example, is the introductory passage from a popular history of the Seattle area — a passage written in the 1940s and reprinted through many editions of a current college anthology:

> The Governor made a fine speech, but he was outranged and outclassed that day. Chief Seattle, who answered on behalf of the Indians, towered a foot above the Governor. He wore his blanket like the toga of a Roman senator, and he did not have to strain his

famous voice, which everyone agreed was audible and distinct at a distance of half a mile.

Seattle's oration was in Duwamish. Doctor Smith, who had learned the language, wrote it down; under the flowery garlands of his translation the speech rolls like an articulate iron engine, grim with meanings that outlasted his generation and may outlast all the generations of men. As the amiable follies of the white race become less amiable, the iron rumble of old Seattle's speech sounds louder and more ominous.

Standing in front of Doctor Maynard's office in the stumpy clearing, with his hand on the little Governor's head, the white invaders about him and his people before him, Chief Seattle [spoke].[1]

Some strong but questionable assertions carry this passage and brush aside problems about where, exactly, the speech could have taken place, in what language it could have been spoken, and how much of any Indian language Smith ever knew. It is true that Smith's own introduction places the speech in Seattle, has Governor Stevens introduced by Dr. David S. Maynard, in front of Maynard's office, and mentions a great gathering of Indians, both in canoes on Elliott Bay and along the shore. Smith also describes Seattle's arising with "the dignity of a senator," placing one hand on the governor's head, and even "pointing heavenward" with the index finger of the other hand. But there is no evidence of his blanket arranged as a toga, of a stumpy clearing, or of a speech by Stevens that was more than "conversational, plain, and straight-

---

1. Binns, 100; reprinted in Eastman, 475, in a section of selections titled "History." In a separate section, "Nature and the Environment," a brief and wholly spurious "Letter to President Pierce by Chief Seattle" is also reprinted, 399–400. This "letter," derived from the Perry film script, is not reprinted in later editions of the Nabakov anthology.

forward" (Smith's words). In short, the suggestions made in Smith's sketch are embellished here (as elsewhere) to make up a symbolic scene, a tableau of figures that personify great forces in conflict.

On one side is an evident Noble Savage, tall, dignified, simply clad, speaking with sonorous authority. On the other side is an evident Petty Official, short in stature, using fine words but without much range or depth. The two stand in a wasteland — the forest of the Indians become the stumpy clearing of the white invaders.

Even heavier sarcasm appears in a headnote to the speech written in the late 1960s. Here the new clearing in the wilderness has resulted from the massive swindle of one people by another: "Behind closed doors it had been decided that [white men] and Indians could never live together in civilized amity; the red men, therefore, would have to be segregated, moved to huge concentration camps politely called 'reservations.'" The rest of Washington Territory was to be purchased at seven cents an acre, with payment to be made over many years, not in cash but in "useful articles."[2] Again, these assertions are not completely accurate, but they set the stage for a prodigious orator to rise and face a villainous smooth talker.

The full implications of the offer seemed to be understood by only one Indian leader, Chief Seattle (c. 1786–1866), "a Titan among Lilliputians," standing "six feet full in his moccasins, broad shouldered, deep chested and finely proportioned," the chief who had

---

2. Lee, 239–40. The Miller and Miller bibliography credits Lee with reprinting the accurate text of the Smith version for the first time since 1891.

recently succeeded in uniting most of the reduced and disparate coastal tribes, and who was to lend his name to the great city of the Northwest....

In 1854 the new governor, West Point soldier and frontiersman Isaac I. Stevens, invited all the tribes in the Puget Sound area to a spectacular powwow to hear about the generous terms of the land purchase. Stevens made a speech of welcome, and in glowing terms outlined the magnanimity in the latest scheme for getting the Indians out of the way. Then it was Chief Seattle's turn to respond. He could remember back — or thought he could — to the coming of Vancouver's ships, the days of the early traders, of Lewis and Clark, Astoria, and the North West Company, and with this perspective had his say in one of the great political addresses of the century — though at least a little of the poetry and tempered cynicism in the speech may be attributed to Seattle linguist Dr. Henry A. Smith, who heard it and translated the sonorous Chinook oratory into English. (Lee, 240)

Again we find a great contrast of characters: on the one hand, a tall chief, finely proportioned, the rightful leader of a large people, who generously "lent" his name to a great city; on the other hand, a governor, soldier, frontiersman — and swindler. Seattle's voice here has a claim to speak for the place. Within the speech itself, this point becomes explicit. Seattle claims to speak for the land and for his ancestors and kinfolk who have inhabited every feature of it, and who will continue to abide there long after Indians have moved away and been supplanted. On the other side, Governor Stevens appears in this scene as a figure exerting many new claims on the land. He had come west, in fact, by leading a major surveying party across the Plains and the Rockies, to map and report a railroad route from the upper Mississippi to Puget Sound. He consciously and eagerly represented new forces that would make the United States a great continental nation. Indeed he fostered the rapidly approaching literal "iron engines" that would ravage the surrounding hills and forests and transform them beyond recognition.

The continuing fascination of Seattle's speech is, therefore, a puzzle about where to put one's loyalties and faith. Is there a voice within the American landscape, whose tones modern Americans can trace, even faintly, in the records of Henry A. Smith — and whose admonitions we ignore at our peril? Or are we inescapably bound to the world of Isaac Stevens, and to the new order of settlement he helped to design and establish at the farthest reaches of the continent?

To put these questions more sharply and effectively, we must turn now to the speech itself, in the full account Smith published in 1887. This material is the essential text for all further discussion, and it should be read through without undue interruption. But even in this earliest form the speech is framed in a tableau. It is not quite the modern contrast of an Indian sage addressing an empire builder, nor is it the even more recently fashionable voice of wilderness speaking out against industrial pollution. These settings can be derived or elaborated from this source and its language very easily, but they are not what Smith has immediately in mind. In Smith's version, Seattle is rather an imposing but doomed orator, a great-souled leader, speaking calmly but forcefully to another great gentleman on an important occasion.

Smith's account was printed in the *Seattle Sunday Star* of October 29, 1887, as the tenth installment of a column he wrote, and its heading suggests that he copied his own diary to celebrate a hero from the past:

Early Reminiscences.
Number Ten.
Scraps from a Diary.
Chief Seattle — A Gentleman by
Instinct — His Native Elo-
quence. Etc., Etc.

Under this heading, Smith takes time to recreate a dramatic and symbolic encounter. Here, in full and without any editorial correction, is his description of what Seattle was like and how he came to speak:

Old Chief Seattle was the largest Indian I ever saw, and by far the noblest looking. He stood six feet full in his moccasins, was broad shouldered, deep chested, and finely proportioned. His eyes were large, intelligent, expressive, and friendly when in repose, and faithfully mirrored the varying moods of the great soul that looked through them. He was usually solemn, silent and dignified, but on great occasions moved among assembled multitudes like a Titian among, Liliputians, and his lightest word was law.

When rising to speak in council or to tender advice, all eyes were turned upon him, and deep-toned, sonorous and eloquent sentences rolled from his lips like the ceaseless thunders of cataracts flowing from exhaustless fountains, and

HIS MAGNIFICENT BEARING

was as noble as that of the most cultivated military chieftain in command of the forces of a continent. Neither his eloquence, his dignity or his grace, were acquired. They were as native to his manhood as leaves and blossoms are to a flowering almond.

His influence was marvelous. He might have been an emperor but all his instincts were democratic, and he ruled his loyal subjects with kindness and paternal benignity.

He was always flattered by marked attention from white men, and never so much as when seated at their tables, and on such occasions he manifested more than anywhere else the genuine instincts of a gentleman.

When Governor Stevens first arrived in Seattle and told the natives he had been appointed commissioner of Indian affairs for Washington Territory, they gave him a demonstrative reception in front of Dr. Maynard's office, near the water front on Main street. The Bay swarmed with canoes and the shore was lined with a living mass of swaying, writhing, dusky humanity, until

OLD CHIEF SEATTLE'S

trumpet-toned voice rolled over the immense multitude, like the startling reveille of a bass drum, when silence became as instantaneous and perfect as that which follows a clap of thunder from a clear sky.

The governor was then introduced to the native multitude by Dr. Maynard, and at once commenced, in a conversational, plain and straightforward style, an explanation of his mission among them, which is too well understood to require recapitulation.

When he sat down, Chief Seattle arose with all the dignity of a senator, who carries the responsibilities of a great nation on his shoulders. Placing one hand on the governor's head, and slowly pointing heavenward with the index finger of the other, he commenced his memorable address in solemn and impressive tones.

At the close of the speech, Smith furnishes one further paragraph about its setting:

Other speakers followed, but I took no notes. Governor Stevens' reply was brief. He merely promised to meet them in general council on some future occasion to discuss the proposed treaty. Chief Seattle's promise to adhere to the treaty should one be ratified, was observed to the letter, for he was ever the unswerving and faithful friend of the white man. The above is but a fragment of his speech, and lacks all the charm lent by the grace and earnestness of the sable old orator, and the occasion.

Between these two sections of Smith's framing, he presents the speech as follows. Unfortunately, there is only one surviving copy of this issue of the *Star*, and it is a damaged sheet with missing or half-legible lines in some places. The speech was reprinted, however, in *History of Seattle, Washington* by Frederick James Grant (433–36). What follows is therefore the text as it appears in the *Star*, with phrases in brackets from the reprint in Grant's *History*.

CHIEF SEATTLE'S SPEECH
The Complete Text of 1887

Yond[er] sky that has wep[t tears] of compassion on our fathers for centuries untold, and which, to us, looks et[erna]l, may change. Today it is fair[, tom]orrow it may be [overca]st with [clou]ds. My [words are like the] stars that never set. What Seattle says, the great chief, Washington, (The Indians in early times thought that Washington was still alive. They knew the name to be that of a president, and when they heard of the president *at* Washington they mistook the name of the city for the name of the reigning chief. They thought, also, that King George was still England's monarch, because the Hudson bay traders called themselves "King George men." This innocent deception the company was shrewd enough not to explain away for the Indians had more respect for them than they would have had, had they known England was ruled by a woman. Some of us have learned better.) can rely upon, with as much certainty as our pale-face brothers can rely upon the return of the seasons.

The son of the white chief says his father sends us greetings of friendship and good will. This is kind, for we know he has little need of our friendship in return, because his people are many. They are like the grass that covers the vast prairies, while my people are few, and resemble the scattering trees of a storm-swept plain.

The great, and I presume also good, white chief sends us word that he wants to buy our lands but is willing to allow us to reserve enough to to live on comfortably. This indeed appears generous, for the red man no longer has rights that he need respect, and the offer may be wise, also, for we are no longer in need of a great country.

THERE WAS A TIME

when our people covered the whole land, as the waves of a wind-ruffled sea cover its shell-paved floor. But that time has long since passed away with the greatness of tribes now almost forgotten. I will not mourn over our untimely decay, nor reproach my pale-face brothers for hastening it, for we, too, may have been some-what to blame.

When our young men grow angry at some real or imaginary wrong, and disfigure their faces with black paint, their hearts, also, are disfigured and turn black, and then their cruelty is re-lentless and knows no bounds, and our old men are not able to re-strain them.

But let us hope that hostilities between the red-man and his pale-face brothers may never return. We would have everything to lose and nothing to gain.

True it is, that revenge, with our young braves, is considered gain, even at the cost of their own l[iv]es, but old men who stay at home [in] times of war, and old women, who have sons to lose, know better.

Our great father Washington, for I presume he is now our father, as well as yours, since George has moved his boundaries to the north; our great and good father, I say, sends us word by his son, who, no doubt, is a great chief among his people, that if we do as he desires, he will protect us. His brave armies will be to us a bristling wall of strength, and his great ships of war will fill our harbors so that our ancient enemies far to the northward, the Simsiams and Hydas, will no longer frighten our women and old men. Then he will be our father and we will be his children.

BUT CAN THIS EVER BE?

Your God loves your people and hates min[e]; he [folds his strong] arms [lovingly around the white man and] leads him as a father leads his infant son, but he has forsaken his red children; he makes your people wax strong every day, and soon they will fill the land; while my people are ebbing away like a fast-receding tide, that will never flow again. The white man's God cannot love his red children or he would protect them. They seem to be orphans and can look nowhere for help. How then can we become brothers? How can your father become our father and bring us prosperity and awaken in us dreams of returning greatness?

Your God seems to us to be partial. He came to the white man. We never saw Him; never even heard His voice; He gave the white man laws but He had no word for His red children whose teeming millions filled this vast continent as the stars fill the firmament. No, we are two distinct races and must ever remain so. There is little in common between us. The ashes of our ancestors are

14

sacred and their final resting place is hallowed ground, while you wander away from the tombs of your fathers seemingly without regret.

Your religion was written on tables of stone by the iron finger of an angry God, lest you might forget it. The red man could never remember nor comprehend it.

Our religion is the traditions of our ancestors, the dreams of our old men, given them by the great Spirit, and the visions of our sachems, and is written in the hearts of our people.

Your dead cease to love you and the homes of their nativity as soon as they pass the portals of the tomb. They wander far off beyond the stars, are soon forgotten, and never return. Our dead never forget the beautiful world that gave them being. They still love its winding rivers, its great mountains and its sequestered vales, and they ever yearn in tenderest affection over the lonely hearted living and often return to visit and comfort them.

Day and night cannot dwell together. The red man has ever fled the approach of the white man, as the changing mists on the mountain side flee before the blazing morning sun.

However, your proposition seems a just one, and I think my folks will accept it and will retire to the reservation you offer them, and we will dwell apart and in peace, for the words of the great white chief seem to be the voice of nature speaking to my people out of the thick darkness that is fast gathering around them like a dense fog floating inward from a midnight sea.

It matters but little where we pass the remainder of our days.

THEY ARE NOT MANY.

The Indian's night promises to be dark. No bright star hovers about the horizon. Sad-voiced winds moan in the distance. Some grim Nemesis of our race is on the red man's trail, and wherever

15

he goes he will still hear the sure approaching footsteps of the fell destroyer and prepare to meet his doom, as does the wounded doe that hears the approaching footsteps of the hunter. A few more moons, a few more winters, and not one of all the mighty hosts that once filled this broad land or that now roam in fragmentary bands through these vast solitudes will remain to weep over the tombs of a people once as powerful and hopeful as your own.

But why should we repine? Why should [I murmur at the] fate of my people? Tribes are made up of individuals and are no better than [th]ey. Men come and go like the waves of the sea. A tear, a tamanawus, a dirge, and they are gone from our longing eyes forever. Even the white man, whose God walked and talked with him, as friend to friend, is not exempt from the common destiny. We *may* be brothers after [all.] We shall see.

We will ponder your proposition, and when we have decided we will tell you. But should we accept it, I here and now make this the first condition: That we will not be denied the privilege, without molestation, of visiting at will the graves of our ancestors and friends. Every part of this country is sacred to my people. Every hill-side, every valley, every plain and grove has been hallowed by some fond memory or some sad experience of my tribe.

EVEN THE ROCKS

that seem to lie dumb as they swelter in the sun along the silent seashore in solemn grandeur thrill with memories of past events connected with the fate of my people, and the very dust under your feet responds more lovingly to our footsteps than to yours, because it is the ashes of our ancestors, and our bare feet are conscious of the sympathetic touch, for the soil is rich with the life of our kindred.

The sable braves, and fond mothers, and glad-hearted maidens, and the little children who lived and rejoiced here, and whose very names are now forgotten, still love these solitudes, and their deep fastnesses at eventide grow shadowy with the presence of dusky spirits. And when the last red man shall have perished from the earth and his memory among white men shall have become a myth, these shores shall swarm with the invisible dead of my tribe, and when your children's children shall think themselves alone in the field, the store, the shop, upon the highway or in the silence of the woods they will not be alone. In all the earth there is no place dedicated to solitude. At night, when the streets of your cities and villages shall be silent, and you think them deserted, they will throng with the returning hosts that once filled and still love this beautiful land. The white man will never be alone. Let him be just and deal kindly with my people, for the dead are not altogether powerless.

CHAPTER 2

The Vanishing Text

THE SOURCE WE HAVE JUST SURVEYED, Henry Smith's column
of 1887, has long seemed to be a confirmed historical document.
Compared to the other versions of the Seattle speech, it claims a
number of distinct advantages. It is the earliest surviving record.
It comes from a direct witness. It dates from a period still early in
the history of what would become Washington State (it was still
Washington Territory in 1887). And it appears in unpretentious
form, as an admittedly incomplete and yet admiring recollection
in a newspaper circulating to other pioneers along Puget Sound. If
one looks closely at the speech itself, this version also reveals
some telltale details that bespeak its naive authenticity. It includes out-of-date terms that have to be explained to a later generation. And the language of the speech sometimes seems to tran-
scend the talents of the author of the column; Seattle's language,
even filtered through Smith's, seems far more nobly direct, coherent, and plangent than the sentimental prose that frames it. It also
stands apart from the other known productions of Smith's pen.

Yet every one of these points in favor of this document can also
be turned to call its authenticity into doubt. It is the oldest surviving record, but it is hardly as old as one could wish: an 1887 publication of an encounter and speech from the early 1850s. It comes
from Smith, who claims to have been on the scene and kept notes
and a diary; but those records have never come to light. There is
no confirmation from any other source that they ever existed; that
Smith was, in fact, present at a meeting between Seattle and Governor Stevens; or that Chief Seattle made such a speech. In any

case, this report is admittedly based on translation. It does not record exactly what Seattle said in his own language; it seems to be worked up from incomplete notes of uncertain date. It filters an Indian oral performance into English and into cold print. It colors Seattle's ideas with Smith's vocabulary and Smith's sense of historical significance. Set against Smith's other writings it may seem strangely, even uniquely, powerful; yet it could also be the curious masterpiece of a writer with grand ambitions and limited talents.

The meaning, accuracy, and authority of this text are also darkened by its appearance in a mere, obscure, evanescent newspaper column. In this form it appeals to the commonplace literacy of nineteenth-century Americans, and to a long tradition of viewing Indians through readers' spectacles. It thus diminishes Seattle's greatest moment into an item of merely passing interest, while at the same time it claims to dramatize Seattle as the towering spokesman of his people and his place. Finally, it reports a kind of speech that we now have to see as typical of white men's prejudices and expectations about Indians: a noble, sad, and moving speech of capitulation in the face of an irresistible invasion.

How are we to balance these various considerations? On the one hand, Smith's account has to remain the irreducible central document about this speech. There is no other text to challenge its language or enable us to see into its sources and composition. However much we might long for earlier notes or independent accounts, none seems likely to appear. Without Smith, there is no Seattle speech. Whatever Seattle said or meant, in word or deed, has to be read through this one tattered page of the *Seattle Star*. On the other hand, a sensitive reader has to sift through layer after layer of doubt. One has to listen carefully for what may be an authentic Indian voice here. Smith may well be reporting some echo or recollection of Puget Sound Indians' protests, even if he is not transcribing one single, connected great speech by a single leader on a high occasion. He may well have had some notes, some pondered memories, and some long-absorbed observations about white invasion to put into his column. It seems improbable that he contrived this whole speech suddenly and from scratch in a week or two of 1887; that line of development does not fit with other evidence, including his other writings. Still, we have to measure Smith's entire account against several frames of reference — as it were, several mattes and frames that make it his and our glazed-over version of a great tableau.

What can we know of the original voice Smith heard or claimed to hear? We can find some teasing clues, but we have to bear in mind that long before Smith's time others had "heard" and read Indian voices and taught others just how to listen. Their example should chasten our confidence.

We must begin with the earliest available evidence, Smith's account and text of the speech in the *Seattle Sunday Star* of October 29, 1887. But even this step is not simple. There is just one surviving copy of that particular issue, now preserved in the Newspapers and Microforms department of the Suzzallo Library at the University of Washington, and that copy is defective. It is a damaged sheet of newsprint; some passages are torn, missing, or indecipherable. Librarians have done their best to reinforce and preserve it, but it is a fragile remnant of an obscure old publication. Around 1980 the surviving issues of the *Star* were microfilmed. A master film at the University of Washington and a copy at the Washington State Library were entered in the *Microforms in Print* supplement of 1981 (*Newspapers in Microform*, 136). But these film copies omit one passage of several lines from the Seattle speech. The lines are covered and blanked out by a piece of translucent reinforcing tape. Fine details are also hard to make out from the copy on film and even from the coarse and aging newsprint of the original sheet. Thus even the exact text of 1887 is now unrecoverable. The best we can do is transcribe the surviving sheet, including the passages covered with tape, and supply missing words or lines from a copy published just a few years later. (This was the editorial procedure behind the reprinting of the text in chapter 1.)

It may seem shocking that a document of such importance has been allowed to perish, so that only one tattered copy survives. But a more balanced view may be that it is fortunate that we have so much. The *Seattle Sunday Star* was not a memorable publication but an ephemeral local paper. Its issues were probably discarded within a few weeks by almost all of its subscribers. Once Grant's *History of Seattle* had reprinted the full text of Smith's article in 1891, it might have seemed pointless for anyone to try to keep the article itself. Certainly no editor, scholarly or otherwise, has gone back to the newspaper copy with sufficient care to point out its evident typographical errors and peculiarities. Until now it seems to have been confidently ignored.

Indeed the history of Smith's article as a text has followed a very different path from its history as an artifact. The text has been copied, embellished, revived, and projected around the world. In effect, it has been resurrected in a completely new form, while the original newspaper sheet has languished in darkness and barely escaped oblivion. These divergent histories make it all the more important that we look again at what Smith actually wrote and how it was first published.

All subsequent versions have distorted the speech in two ways. They have presented an inaccurate or incomplete text, and yet they have padded it out with some apparatus or claims of scholarly respectability. Important reprintings in 1891, 1931, and 1969 have made both kinds of distortion and fostered other mistaken views of this text. We must take a moment to look at these developments and set them aside, before we can see Smith's article on its own terms.

Frederick James Grant's *History of Seattle* appeared in 1891, while Henry Smith was still alive, and it reprinted Smith's entire account (433–36). This version corrected a few printing errors from the *Star*, but it introduced others. It leaves out the word "that," for example, in the opening line of the speech: "Yonder sky that has wept tears of compassion" (434). And when Seattle speaks, sentences roll from his lips like the "ceaselsss [*sic*] thunders of cataracts" (433). Grant's version probably saved Smith's account from oblivion, by transferring a simple newspaper column into a sturdy volume of "history." It is from Grant, not from the *Star*, that almost all later reprintings have derived. Yet it should be noted that the *History* prints the speech as a kind of appended note — not in the chapter on early settlement but in the long final chapter "Men of Seattle," as part of the biographical entry on Henry A. Smith. On balance, this version trades one set of typographical errors for another, and transmutes the authority of a "reminiscence" into the equally dubious authority of a tribute to local pioneers. In fact, it seems to absorb Chief Seattle into a supporting role in Smith's biography, for there is no biographical entry for Seattle himself or any other Indian leader. Grant thus preserves the speech as authentic but very marginal to developments after the 1850s.

In the early 1930s three regional writers published new versions based on Grant's, and thus revitalized the meaning of the speech in different ways. Roberta Frye Watt, the granddaughter of a pioneer, wrote *The Story of Seattle* (also titled *Four Wagons West*) in 1931, and included a much-altered version of the speech (pp.

179–82). John M. Rich brought out a pamphlet devoted to the speech in 1932, *Chief Seattle's Unanswered Challenge*. And in 1931 Clarence B. Bagley included the speech in a scholarly article, "Chief Seattle and Angeline," in *Washington Historical Quarterly*. It is hard to say which of these publications carried the most weight; all three brought the speech into notice again, and with different emphases. Whatever the shortcomings of Watt's research or editing, she seems to have been the first writer to present Seattle's speech in the main narrative of a popular local history. Rich's little book stressed the deep and universal spiritual message of the speech — anticipating the ecology movement by about forty years. And Bagley's article seemed to give the speech the authority of modern scholarly research. It brought together much information and for years was regarded as *the* expert account of Chief Seattle's life; it is cited, for example, as the leading source about him in *Dictionary of American Biography*. At the time he wrote his article, Bagley was president of the state historical society, which published the *Quarterly*. He had also published a three-volume history of Seattle, in 1916 — which did not mention Chief Seattle's speech, though it did have a substantial biographical entry on Henry Smith.

One might hope that with this background Bagley would take scrupulous care to present a new account that was accurate in every detail. Yet he misdates Smith's publication by ten years (1877 instead of 1887) and presents a text that has been altered from earlier sources and notably embellished. In both the Smith and Grant versions, Seattle speaks the following final sentences: "The white man will never be alone. Let him be just and deal kindly with my people, for the dead are not altogether powerless" (Smith's version has a typographical error: "altogother"). Bagley has "The White Man will never be alone," but then, perhaps following Rich, he adds a new paragraph: "Let him be just and deal kindly with my people, for the dead are not powerless. Dead — I say? There is no death. Only a change of worlds" (Bagley, 255). On the authority of Bagley's publication, these words have closed the speech in numerous reprints — though many have emended "Dead — I say?" to "Dead — did I say?" [1]

The famous modern versions of the speech — put together by William Arrowsmith and Ted Perry — also make peculiar modifications of Seattle's words. When Arrowsmith prepared his text in the late 1960s, he was a professor of classics at the University of Texas, well known for his many translations of ancient plays. He first published the Seattle speech in 1969 and presented it as another work of translation, in *Arion: A Journal of the Humanities and Classics*. He provided footnotes to clarify some points in the text and ended with two lines in parentheses: "Translated from the Victorian English of Dr. Henry Smith of Seattle, published in the *Seattle Star* on October 29, 1877 [*sic*]." In 1973 Arrowsmith published the same text again, in *American Poetry Review*. This time he wrote a headnote, explaining that his aim "was to strip away the disfiguring white rhetoric of Smith . . . in order to reveal the lines and movement of what I regard as a basically authentic speech" (10). Arrowsmith's account of the speech, however, was glaringly inaccurate and inconsistent. He claimed, for example, that Seattle was speaking not to Governor Stevens but to other

---

1. Rich puts this passage in italics at the end of the speech, also in a separate paragraph: *"Dead — did I say? There is no death. Only a change of worlds!"* (Rich, 41). His version is embellished in many other passages, as well. The influence of Watt, Rich, and Bagley on each other is impossible to untangle. See Krenmayr, 4–6, for the suggestion that Rich was the principal tinkerer with the final lines of the speech.

Indians "in a mainly Indian council which was no part of the official negotiations." His version opens with the words, "Brothers: That sky above us has pitied our fathers for many hundreds of years." Later in the speech, however, there are long passages that contrast "us" and "you," where "us" clearly refers to Indians and "you" refers to "you white men." In short, Arrowsmith claimed to see through what he called "Smith's fustian version" or "the dense patina of white literary rhetoric"; but in fact he had to rely on Smith as "the *only* source" anyone could use, he followed Smith closely at many points, and he freely distorted or denied the information in Smith's account.

Ted Perry's version derived directly from Arrowsmith's. Perry later explained to Rudolph Kaiser that he was inspired by Arrowsmith's reading of the speech at the first Earth Day observance in 1970. Over the course of the following year he prepared a film script about ecology based on this material. The resulting television film, entitled "Home," was first aired on the ABC network in 1972. Perry also claimed that he never intended to pass his work off as authentic, as the actual historical words of Chief Seattle. This seems odd, for several reasons. In his letter to Kaiser, Perry himself went on to say that he secured Arrowsmith's permission before he set to work.[2] In a separate account, Arrowsmith recalled that he insisted on approving the results.[3] Finally, there is the evidence of the text itself. It plainly purports to be a speech by Chief Seattle, in printed versions that seem to have had Perry's approval. Passages such as the following appear in both the full text quoted by Kaiser in 1987 and another text published with Perry's byline in 1989:

---

2. Ted Perry to Rudolph Kaiser, Nov. 11, 1983, quoted in Kaiser, 514.

3. William Arrowsmith to Carl Ross, January 20, 1978, quoted in Kaiser, 513.

What Chief Seattle says, the Great Chief in Washington can count on as surely as our white brothers can count on the return of the seasons. My words are like the stars. They do not set.

Chief Washington also sends us words of friendship and good-will. This is kind of him.

So we will consider your offer to buy our land. It will not be easy. This land is sacred to us.[4]

In 1992 Perry again protested that he, and not Seattle, was the author of this version, when it was illustrated by Susan Jeffers and turned into a best-selling children's book, *Brother Eagle, Sister Sky*. The publishers retorted that, in effect, they were reproducing a widely known version of Seattle's language and violating no copyrights.[5]

By the mid-1970s there were thus four or five competing, yet seemingly authoritative different versions of this text, and variations were beginning to proliferate in broadcasts, posters, and reprints. As we have seen, Rudolph Kaiser untangled much confusion in his scholarly article on the subject in 1987. He explained that the speeches written by Arrowsmith and Perry were different from each other and very different from texts reprinted from Smith, Grant, Rich, or Bagley. He secured recollections by Perry and Arrowsmith about how their versions came to be written, and

4. Perry, 29; Kaiser, 525–26, prints similar lines in a very different full text. The 1989 version was published in *Middlebury College Magazine* while Perry was a professor at Middlebury.

5. Mary Murray, 103. The last, unnumbered page of *Brother Eagle, Sister Sky* explains that its text derives from the speech as quoted by Joseph Campbell in a television series with Bill Moyers, which was reprinted in *The Power of Myth*. Campbell's quotation is a brief, much-edited version of Perry's text (Campbell, 34–35).

he printed full texts for comparison. Nevertheless, when he came to judge the merits of these different texts, Kaiser wavered, too, and perhaps contributed to further confusion. In the end, he greatly admired the speech that Ted Perry wrote for television! He surveyed its many reprintings and the discussion it provoked in Europe and around the world, and tried to explain its strong appeal:

> The imagery, the symbolism, the phrasing, and the wording [of this version] seem to be in perfect unison with its purpose and its message on the one hand, and with the wishes, the concerns, and the expectations of many people on the other hand.... Whoever wrote these words, they constitute an impressive piece of writing. It is easy to see that such words may well function as a mythical or religious statement.... [The] idea that each and every thing and creature in this world is spiritual and sacred, may well prove to be the salient point of this text, salient for a society which has always neatly separated the temporal and the spiritual and in this way has tried to justify man's claim that all the non-sacred world is at his disposal. (Kaiser, 516–17)

Should this praise be directed to Perry, or to Perry in the guise of Chief Seattle? Kaiser is vague on this point. He seems to want it both ways. Perry derives what he says from Chief Seattle, yet he has authored a wholly new composition. It is a misleading corruption of a text, yet a brilliant modern testament. Words that take their force from a dramatic script, in the voice of a revered Indian leader, nonetheless take their force from their sensitivity alone, or their articulation of a much-needed idea. "This text does not represent the mind of the old Chief, but the mind of a sensitive Euro-American, worried about our ecological situation and the general dualism of our culture. The text of the speech is, therefore, valid; but the claim that Chief Seattle was its author certainly is 'spurious'" (Kaiser, 517–18). This is Kaiser's concluding judgment.

After several stages of transmission and scholarly editing, therefore, the speech remains clouded in doubtful texts and confused appraisals. In various inaccurate forms it has been circulating for a generation, not only in the popular press but also in university courses in American history and literature. Thanks in part to Kaiser's article, some recent textbook editions have dropped the speech or added cautionary notes about its origins. But it is still featured in others, as an authentic voice crying out of the wilderness of the American past.[6]

When set against this modern foreground of textual tinkering and distortion, the old page of the *Star* has a refreshing crudeness and simplicity. It seems to be just what it is and no more: a pioneer's recollections, rescued from old notes or a diary and written out in admittedly sketchy and incomplete form. The paper is rough, the typesetting hasty, the author a mere local columnist with a tale worth preserving. "Scraps from a Diary," reads the headline. "Other speakers followed, but I took no notes," the writer concludes. Smith implies that he has definite written sources, or notes still at hand, but he admits they are not adequate. "The above is but a fragment of his speech, and lacks all the charm lent by the grace and earnestness of the sable old orator, and the occasion."

---

6. The speech has been reprinted, for example, in Paul Lauter, et al., eds., *The Heath Anthology of American Literature* (1990, 1:1769–72; omitted from the second ed., 1994); Donald McQuade, et al., eds., *The Harper American Literature* (2d ed., 1993), 2:227; James E. Miller, Jr., ed., *Heritage of American Literature* (1991), 1:1955. All three anthologies reprint embellished texts from the 1930s.

Other modest, unsophisticated, even awkward touches appear in this text and work to affirm its authenticity. One is the intrusion of a long explanatory note, to help later readers understand an anachronism. Another is the casual use of an untranslatable Indian expression.

In the very first paragraph of the speech, Smith interrupts the flow of a sentence with a parenthesis of several lines. It makes no editorial sense to have such an intrusion at this point. Smith has just introduced the speech as a "memorable address in solemn and impressive tones" delivered in a striking scene, with Seattle towering over the governor and "pointing heavenward." The speech begins with four rolling sentences about eternity, change, and human promises. But then, just as Seattle comes to the main point — that his word is as steadfast as the stars — Smith throws in a mundane history lesson:

> My words are like the stars that never set. What Seattle says, the great chief, Washington (The Indians in early times thought that Washington was still alive. They knew the name to be that of a president, and when they heard of the president *at* Washington they mistook the name of the city for the name of the reigning chief. They thought, also, that King George was still England's monarch, because the Hudson bay traders called themselves "King George men." This innocent deception the company was shrewd enough not to explain away for the Indians had more respect for them than they would have had, had they known England was ruled by a woman. Some of us have learned better.) can rely upon, with as much certainty as our pale face brothers can rely upon the return of the seasons.

Obviously something has gone awry here. Most likely, Smith wrote out this explanatory note as some kind of appendage to the copy he prepared for the press. It could have been an intended foot-note, an added slip of paper, or a marginal notation. But someone — an editor, the compositor who set the column in type, Smith himself in a lapse while revising his manuscript — placed this ex-planation between parenthesis marks and clumsily shoved it right here, between subject and verb, to make a mess of the "solemn and impressive tones" that Smith has just promised to introduce.

Could such a clumsy lapse be deliberate? Could Smith have ar-ranged this homely slip on purpose, to make a conspicuous point of his artlessness? That seems a very far-fetched explanation. This particular note matches Smith's pompous and rather knowing tone; it seems of a piece with what he writes elsewhere in his own voice. Suppose the worst: that Smith completely fabricated the Se-attle speech and then devised one or two touches to cover his forgery. Would this be one such touch? Would he make himself out as an editorial pedant, with the long-range aim of sustaining Seattle's noble bearing? Such a tactic hardly makes sense in this particular paragraph, for it detracts from Seattle's dignity, even makes him appear rather ignorant, right at the start of his speech.

But if this parenthesis is not a deliberate blunder, it implies that the speech is very distinct from the framework Smith pro-vides for it. At the very least, it implies that his column contains at least three separate compositions: Seattle's speech; Smith's narra-tive about the speech, speaker, and occasion; and this parentheti-cal remark. Smith may have completely devised all three, but if he were consummately crafty about it he could have blended the third element much better with either of the other two. Instead, the balance of probabilities is that he is presenting just what he claims, a speech pieced together from old notes along with an ac-count of its circumstances and a footnote about an odd expres-sion (which he now realizes needs a gloss).

Besides, this parenthetical note happens to be accurate about circumstances in the 1850s and to be a helpful gloss for other lines in the speech.

A later passage also mentions "Washington" for the United States government and "George" for the British Empire, and contains further touches that accurately reflect the historical situation:

> Our great father Washington, for I presume he is now our father, as well as yours, since George has moved his boundaries to the north; our great and good father, I say, sends us word by his son, who, no doubt, is a great chief among his people, that if we do as he desires, he will protect us. His brave armies will be to us a bristling wall of strength, and his great ships of war will fill our harbors so that our ancient enemies far to the northward, the Simsiams and Hydas, will no longer frighten our women and old men. Then he will be our father and we will be his children.

The British and United States governments *had* recently moved the international boundary to the north. By the Oregon treaty, ratified by the Senate in June 1846, the mainland boundary was fixed at the 49th parallel and the Hudson's Bay Company had moved its main post from the Columbia River to Vancouver Island. Moreover, raids of northern Indians into Puget Sound were a matter of concern in this period. Governor Stevens did hold out protection by the United States government as one of the advantages of the treaties he offered.

Again, are these fortuitous or carefully plotted details that Smith culled from local records and dropped into his fabrication? They seem more likely to be unobtrusive features that date from the time he says they do.

Finally, the third paragraph from the end contains a word of

Chinook Jargon, the amalgam of French, English, Spanish, and Indian languages that was used as a trading language in this period. It is such an odd expression in this context that it has not been accurately transcribed in subsequent copies: "Men come and go like the waves of the sea. A tear, a tamanawus, a dirge, and they are gone from our longing eyes forever." If Smith meant to note this word — "tamanawus" — as an authenticating detail in this speech, surely he should have called attention to it. He could have explained it in a parenthesis, as he explains "Washington" and "George." He could have italicized it, as he italicizes the word "may" a few lines later: "We *may* be brothers after all." But he does no such thing. The word is left so inconspicuously on the page that Grant simply miscopied it, as "tamanamus," in 1891. Bagley claims to copy Grant, but changes the wording entirely at this point and omits the expression. W. Storrs Lee reprints the word but puts it in italics, in a different spelling: "A tear, a *tomanawos*, a dirge, and they are gone from our longing eyes forever" (Lee, 243). Lee provides no note or explanation. Watt omits this sentence; Rich and Kaiser have "tamanamus," following Grant. The word has slipped past almost every editor's notice since its original publication, but it was a common expression in Chinook Jargon, which was widely used around Puget Sound in the 1850s. Perhaps this means that Seattle used some words of Chinook Jargon.[7] Or perhaps it means that Smith heard and recorded the translation

---

7. A recent study notes that Chinook Jargon was not just a convenient pidgin language, but also a language many Indians knew and used fluently throughout the region. By 1841 at one trading post along the Columbia River some children seemed to be learning it as their mother tongue; late in the century Franz Boas recorded Chinook jargon poems composed by Indians in British Columbia. See Brown, 86–101, esp. 91–92, 95–97, and 99–100.

of Seattle's speech into the Jargon, or at least recognized the un-translatable idea this word expressed.

The word still presents difficulties to anyone who tries to look it up. Edward Thomas's Chinook Jargon dictionary defines *tah-manawis* as "a guardian or familiar spirit in its personal application." The entry goes on to explain further ranges of meaning: "Every Indian has his tahmanawis. Tahmanawis also means magic, ghost, spirit, or anything supernatural, and is used as the equivalent of luck, fortune and kindred words. It was applied to anything the Indians could not understand" (Thomas, 97–98). The term thus seems to fall into a range of meanings we cover with words such as *spirit, magic, medicine,* and *mystery.* But none of these meanings fits very well with the way this word appears in Smith's sentence. The terms that immediately surround it — "a tear . . . a dirge" — may seem explanatory appositions. But according to Thomas, a *tahmanawis* is not an expression of sadness, as is a tear or a dirge. It is also contradictory to think that a guardian or familiar spirit simply disappears forever, or comes and goes as evanescently as tears or the waves of the sea. The word seems an undigested intrusion in this sentence, perhaps a word heard at the time and jotted down, but not yet properly incorporated into the full sense of the passage. Again, this could well be a mark of clumsiness and rough notetaking from an Indian's speech rather than of Smith's polishing of his own work of noble eloquence.

In fact, it is very odd that Smith puts no special stress on this term. Here if anywhere, he ought to explain a strange expression. *Tahmanawis* or *tahmanaos* describes a complex range of religious ideas and practices of Puget Sound Indians. *Tahmanawis* could mean not only a mystery but a particular kind of ritual. Many observers heard the word used in this way over the years. Myron Eells, for example, lived as a missionary among Puget Sound Indi-

34

ans for many years in the nineteenth century. He wrote about religious and ceremonial life in several chapters about "tamahnous,"
though his modern editor notes that he misunderstood the complex practices he lumped under this single label.[8] The anthropologist Franz Boas conducted his research in Chinook Jargon
throughout this region and took a particular interest in native
languages. He traced the term to the language of the Chinook Indians of the Columbia River, who used it to designate "beings en-
dowed with supernatural power." Boas also explains that it came
to mean "shamanistic acts and all the performances belonging to
the secret societies of the North Pacific coast" (Boas, in Hodge,
2:681). This usage of *tahmanawis* to denote a ritual or secret ceremony fits well with the idea of funeral rites or gestures in "a tear,
a tamanawus, a dirge."

In fact, the term used in this way may be an important clue to
the meaning of the entire speech. It is not just an indication of
Smith's clumsiness and inadvertence, but an extremely significant
word, mediating between the languages of Indians and white invaders, touching the deepest themes of Seattle's protest. In its
large design, the speech addresses white invaders with a deep and
moving sense of permanence and change. The invaders live by a
very different understanding of what is sacred. They have come,
abandoning their own homes, to dislodge a people who have inhabited the region so fully that every hill, valley, plain, and grove
has been hallowed by fond memories. The time has come for Indians to depart and face their nemesis. But the spirits of these
people will remain:

---

8. Eells, xv. Castile cites two modern anthropological studies of Indian
ceremonials: Elmendorf, *The Structure of Twana Culture*; Amoss, *Coast
Salish Spirit Dancing*.

When the last red man shall have perished from the earth and his
memory among white men shall have become a myth, these shores
shall swarm with the invisible dead of my tribe, and when your
children's children shall think themselves alone in the field, the
store, the shop, upon the highway or in the silence of the woods
they will not be alone. In all the earth there is no place dedicated to
solitude. At night, when the streets of your cities and villages shall
be silent and you think them deserted, they will throng with the
returning hosts that once filled and still love this beautiful land.
The white man will never be alone.

The main theme of the speech is not reverence for the land or
the environment — as modern ecologists would have it — but the
persistence and immanence of tribal spirits, even after a temporal
change that may well annihilate the people who have long lived in
the region. Instead of being a mere casual intrusion, the term
tahmanawis thus reflects these spiritual realities in Indian life.
Mysterious guardian spirits will endure and continue to cherish
or haunt the place long after the upheavals of invasion by other
people with other gods. This is a touching passage, and also a
prophecy that should seem powerful or threatening to a settler
such as Smith himself — not a matter of easily dismissed fine
words from an extinct old predecessor.

Smith seems unaware of this power, however, even strangely
obtuse to the language he celebrates. David Buerge, a local historian who has long studied the Seattle speech, finds such eloquence far beyond the powers Smith displayed in his other compositions. Buerge writes:

In the course of his life, he published many articles about the history of the Puget Sound region and wrote a number of poems. A
writer of florid prose, Smith enjoyed telling romantic tales and im-

bued his work with a sense of murky twilight as he bore witness to the passing of the frontier. His poetry was dreadful. The conspicuous quality of Chief Seattle's speech, easily the best thing Smith ever wrote, suggests to me that its strength and imagery derive from what Smith heard rather than from his own talent. (Buerge, "Seattle's King Arthur," 27–28)

Certainly the speech has a different order of eloquence from the introductory passages of Smith's article. Yet one must pause in the face of other evidence, too. The speech seems to fit exactly the "sense of murky twilight" at the passing from one world into another that Buerge notes in Smith's other writings, and Buerge brings in other considerations in his assessment of the speech, too. He reports that Smith could have learned Chinook Jargon just from reading the territorial newspaper of the early 1850s, the *Columbian*. On October 22, 1853, the paper also carried an anonymous article about the immortal dead, from which Buerge quotes: "How unchanging is their love for us. . . . How tenderly they look down upon us and how closely they surround us" (28).

Indeed, Smith could have drawn on a variety of sources. There were accounts and vocabularies of Chinook Jargon in print long before 1887, dating in fact from Joel Palmer's and Horatio Hale's work in the 1840s (Brown, 91-92). And for the idea of ancestral spirits haunting Indian lands, there was a great manifesto against white invasion, published in the *North American Review* in 1879 as a speech by Chief Joseph of the Nez Perce. In that speech or statement, which Joseph is reported to have made in Washington, D.C., he recalled that his father had refused to sign Governor Stevens's treaties. In his dying days, the father staked out the land belonging to his people and summoned his son to his deathbed. There he enjoined the young Joseph never to give up or sell his country:

"You must stop your ears whenever you are asked to sign a treaty selling your home. A few years more, and white men will be all around you. They have their eyes on this land. My son, never forget my dying words. This country holds your father's body. Never sell the bones of your father and mother." Joseph goes on in his own words: "I buried him in that beautiful valley of winding waters. I love that land more than all the rest of the world. A man who would not love his father's grave is worse than a wild animal."[9]

These parallels could have been ingredients ready at hand for a pastiche of Indian oratory. And Buerge emphasizes other points of lore that might have been known or collected by an early Washington settler such as Smith. Puget Sound Indians did believe in a commerce between the living and the dead; they held midwinter ceremonials to recapture kidnapped souls; and in the early nineteenth century they had suffered devastating diseases, with great loss of life, following the arrival of European and American explorers and settlers. "The chaos resulting from depopulation produced religious leaders who prophesied the imminent return of the dead" (Buerge, 28).

How much of the *Seattle Star* speech is translation? How much is Smith's own composition? We are certainly stuck with the shape of Henry Smith obtruding between us and every hint of another voice. And the figure Smith presents elsewhere is not very reassuring. If he was long burdened with the message of Chief Seattle, it did not much affect his behavior as a settler, for he bought up large tracts of land for himself until, around the time of

---

9. Joseph, 417–19. The origins of this text are also suspicious; the article itself does not explain exactly where, when, and under what circumstances Joseph prepared and presented this complete history of his people, or how it found its way into the pages of the *North American Review*.

this publication, he was paying the largest annual property-tax bill in King County.[10] Grant's *History of Seattle* notes that Smith developed property around Smith's Cove on Elliott Bay because he had cannily surveyed Puget Sound to determine the precise spot where the transcontinental railroad would have to reach the Pacific (Grant, 86), though in later sketches Grant and Bagley attribute his place of settlement to his poetic love of natural beauty (Grant, 432; Bagley, *History*, 2:847).

In the *Seattle Sunday Star* of November 5, Smith wrote again about Chief Seattle, in a piece displaying his talents for poetry and celebration. This example of Smith's work is the only other surviving column of his "Reminiscences"; it reinforces all the worst aspects of his earlier presentation. It is a miscellaneous column, noting names and brief histories of other King County pioneers, including two or three hermits and other odd characters. Smith also goes into the naming of local lakes and landmarks, and at this point, he returns to his pompous presentation of the "grand old chief." "Seattle, everyone knows, was named in honor of the grand old chief of collossal [*sic*] frame and courtly bearing, a sylvan monarch without a crewn [*sic*], who was called by Governor Stevens the 'Cicero of the Sound.'" Without further explanation or elaboration of these epithets, Smith then bursts into song. He fills inches of his column with an awkward poem about the name Seattle and its promise of great things to come. Here is the poem, complete and unabridged except for one or two typographical corrections:

---

10. Bagley, *History of Seattle*, 2:849. David Buerge notes the financial and other misfortunes that overcame Smith late in life; he also traces his land deals, gold prospecting, and work among the Indians of Snohomish County after 1863 (Buerge, "Hail to the Chief," 19–24).

SEATTLE

There's a ring and a rhythmical rattle,
　　A clatter of arrows and spears,
In the sybylline name of Seattle,
　　An echo from long buried years.

And the chieftain from whom it descended
　　Was portly, and massive, and tall,
And many a white man befriended,
　　When the hand-writing showed on the wall.

Thus it is that the name is a nomen
　　Cabalistic of friendship and battle,
The fittingest kind of an omen
　　For the Fate-chartered city — Seattle.

And it may be a symbol just hinting
　　Of struggles in store for her sons,
When her harbors and hills shall be glinting
　　And gleaming with sabres and guns.

When the mystical name talismanic,
　　Oft the signal for glory before,
Will nerve them for valor Titanic
　　To hurl back the foe from her shore,

For a name sometimes turns to a slogan,
　　And stands as a symbol of right,
As once did the name of great Logan,
　　That led in the van of the fight.

There's an ominous jingle in "attle,"
　　That gets in one's head and one's heart

And gives him that push and that rattle
  That gave our young city its start.

Some think that we call it *Sea*-ttle
  Because it sits by the sea-side,
And its ships make our merchant's "tin" rattle,
  As they come floating in on the tide.

But that's a mistake, I am certain,
  For its old name could never be mended,
And when it has rung up Fate's curtain,
  We'll see what the gods have intended.

For time, that sets everything right, sir,
  With those who have courage to battle,
Will keep every Seattleite, sir,
  Brim full of the right kind of rattle.

And there's one thing the world can rely on,
  It's a city to do and to dare,
It will grow from a cub to a lion,
  And, lion-like, get the big share.

Even now, to keep step with Seattle,
  All indolent ties one must sever,
And make all the diamond days rattle
  With Spartan and dauntless endeavor.

Yes, a right fitting name is Seattle.
  Seattle forever then be it.
And when it gets under full rattle
  The whole world will stand up to see it!

41

Dreadful as it is, this poem nicely fits the explicit policies of the *Seattle Sunday Star*. In the first issue the editors spelled out their hopes that Seattle would grow to be a great seaport, and their enterprise would succeed as "a literary and society paper wherein the social doings of the week shall be faithfully chronicled, and a judicious selection of literary matters will be presented for the delectation of our readers" (Nov. 11, 1883, p. 2). Regular columns in the surviving issues are titled "Scintillations," "Society Matters," "For the Ladies," "Pilferings," "Local Lyrics," and "The Poet's Corner." Smith's verses are certainly not out of place in this general scheme. But David Buerge is also right that the speech of Chief Seattle is far nobler than Smith's poetry, if this is a typical example.[11]

Many people write terrible poetry, especially occasional, patriotic, newspaper poetry, without knowing how self-indulgent and preposterous they have become. Perhaps in his earlier column Smith was in his right senses and doing his best to report, with some embellishments, the gist of a speech he earlier had heard and taken notes from.

Even so, this poem reveals a certain obtuseness in Smith and his usual readers. It forces us to wonder how intently he could have listened to an Indian speech and whether he could have reported one without resorting to stereotypes. Smith is not known for any other work of Indian translation. Even though as a physician he treated Indians, he had no evident practice or highly developed skill at learning and reporting Indian language and cultural understanding. And in engaging in translation, he recreated a composition in new terms, to fit what his readers could most

---

11. Smith's daughter reported that at his death he left six ledger volumes of verse. McDonald, "Pioneer Doctor," 3.

easily comprehend. He had to use conventions of common modern English with its cultural presuppositions. He had to reconsider his notes (if any) with his recollections of the central ideas and coherence of the speech, its occasion, and its significance over time.

If Chief Seattle did in fact address Isaac I. Stevens, the speech must have passed through interpreters as Smith heard it. It is possible, even likely, that it was interpreted first into Chinook Jargon and then into English. But in Smith's hands it underwent another major translation, from oral performance to written record and printed publication. It thus left the realm of oral, tribal society, and became fixed in very different conventions — conventions that make sense to very modern people, readers who, over the course of the last three centuries, have become habituated to reading newspapers.

These conventions include ways of looking at Indians, recording their appearance, and representing their speech and exotic beliefs.

To see a classic example, we can turn to the often-reprinted *Tatler* and *Spectator* papers of the early eighteenth century. Four Iroquois "kings" were brought to London in 1710 and introduced at the court of Queen Anne. Their visit provoked dozens of literary exercises in the very earliest age of popular newspapers, including *Tatler* no. 171 and *Spectator* nos. 50 and 56 by Joseph Addison and Richard Steele. In *Spectator* no. 56, Addison presents a fictitious account of Indian spiritual beliefs:

> The *Americans* believe that all Creatures have Souls, not only Men and Women, but Brutes, Vegetables, nay even the most inanimate things, as Stocks and Stones. They believe the same of all the Works of Art, as of Knives, Boats, Looking-glasses: And that as any

43

of these things perish, their souls go into another World, which is inhabited by the Ghosts of Men and Women. (Addison and Steele, 1:236)

This paper goes on to report an account of a visit to the realm of the dead, an account secured through interpreters from one of the visiting Indian kings.

In other words, looking to Indians for exotic spiritual depths is a very old story, and along with it comes the very old practice of making an exotic figure the spokesman for ironic or satiric reflections on supposedly civilized ways. Jonathan Swift complained about *Spectator* no. 50 that using an Indian to write observations about England was *his* idea, which he regretted mentioning to Steele: "I repent he ever had it. I intended to have written a book on that subject" (Swift, 1:254–55). (This was a dozen years before Swift published *Gulliver's Travels*.)

Thus the Indian appeared in print early as a wise or naive figure for satire. He also appeared very often as a great public speaker, a noble savage distinguished for his oratory against a backdrop of doom. Very recent critical attention has focussed on records of Indian oratory to bring out this perplexing reflection of translators' preconceptions and projections. David Murray's book *Forked Tongues* devotes a chapter to such projections, many of which show up in Smith's account of Seattle's speech. Following a point made by Hayden White, Murray notes that the term "noble savage" symbolizes a significant historical change. Aboriginal peoples were being driven off the land at the same time that the European ideal of nobility was giving way to bourgeois values. "When applied to North America this idea may give us some idea of the *popularity* of surrender and protest speeches by Indians. In what became a well-used scenario Americans created a public space where could be acted out the renunciation of power by a nobility which was doomed by the very *fact* of its nobility" (David Murray, 36). In short, nobility was dying at the same time that aboriginals were being extirpated, and a simple formula enhanced the drama of both extinctions: the more noble, the more doomed. Murray cites examples of such scenarios in many recorded Indian speeches and in European and American stage plays of the eighteenth and nineteenth centuries.

The scenario calls for the Indian to address a group and act symbolically as a representative leader. Indians are typically represented as almost incapable of speech in private. White readers expect them to speak only dramatically, on one great occasion, when they publicly submit to the advance of exploration and settlement. The texts of such translated and recorded speeches

> have been produced for, and shaped by, the cultural expectations of a white *readership*, but the Indian speech is presented in a dramatic context which has the effect of making it already over-determined for the white reader. As a result the speakers are "framed," so that *what* they are saying is actually less important than the fact and manner of their saying it. This, I would suggest, is one way of explaining the appetite for speeches whose *content* offered an often devastating criticism of white actions. Even as the Indians nobly and eloquently complained, that very nobility and eloquence was confirming the inevitability of their disappearance. (Ibid 36; emphases in original)

By this standard the important message of Seattle's speech is that he agrees in principle to Governor Stevens's treaty proposal. His remarks about American deceptions, follies, or delusions constitute a secondary message, at best — or one that reinforces the primary message by stressing the impossible, doomed nobility of a speaker who judges the grasping ways of the invaders.

Murray mentions the Seattle speech as a good example of this oft-repeated scenario (38), then makes some further turns of the screw. In many of these dramatic speeches, the noble Indian is a spokesman or synecdoche for nature — a voice that speaks on behalf of the landscape itself (41). What endures after the speech has been recorded is a precious noble artifact — a suggestive relic of the last living voice from a bygone time. "The aesthetic power of the speeches is dependent on our being told that this is only a pale imitation, so that the frame, the context, is crucial in determining our response" (43). That frame is the dramatic moment when the noble Indian agreed to vanish.

In light of all these considerations, the text of Seattle's speech presents an opaque or reflective surface to any reader who tries to see into it. Even if we push away the drapery of modern translations and revisions and scrape away the encrustations and distortions of many editors, the best text we can find is a crudely printed page that traces the outline of a symbolic stereotype. It may be that Henry Smith was moved to publish this speech because he did recall an actual Indian voice or Indian voices. But it is also reasonable to ascribe his performance to less inspiring sources: to hints from the territorial *Columbian* newspaper in the 1850s, to the literary conventions of his time, to his general experience of living in Seattle between 1853 and 1887, and not least to the opportunity to focus his talents on a supreme dramatic scenario. In the figure of Chief Seattle he could record the protest and capitulation of one of the very last chiefs, one at the utmost extremity of the American Far West.

CHAPTER 3

The Vanishing Setting

SO FAR WE HAVE TRACED a literary or textual problem and arrived at a tenuous conclusion. There is a very thin thread of possibility that Henry A. Smith actually heard and recorded some kind
of speech by Chief Seattle in front of Isaac I. Stevens on a great
public occasion at the Seattle waterfront. But if this was a historical event, there should be historical evidence of it. There ought to
be some historical moment when that encounter was possible,
and it is hard to pin one down. There are three definite dates when
Stevens visited the village of Seattle or the Seattle area and con-
ferred with local Indians. One other date has been proposed. But
for none of these occasions are there other records that fully confirm the speech Smith reports. Other records of Stevens's travels
and councils are sharply at odds with what Smith has written. So
are other records of Chief Seattle's speeches. One or another of
these dates *may* fit with a great speech by Seattle or another
leader, but none squares very well with the speech Smith reports
or his recollection of its circumstances. Worse yet, in the records
of this period Seattle and Stevens do not appear as mighty oppo-
sites. The stark tableau of Smith's account and later versions of
the speech simply cannot be found. It has to yield to complex
realities about both these men and any setting they may have
shared.

Governor Stevens first reached Puget Sound on November 25,
1853. He and Seattle signed (or made a witnessed mark) on the
treaty of Port Elliott over a full year later, on January 22, 1855.

Stevens was away from Washington Territory on a trip back to the East Coast, from March to December, 1854. That leaves an interval between early December 1853 and March 1854, and a shorter interval between early December 1854 and late January 1855, during which Seattle and Stevens might have met. In both periods Stevens was active with many duties. Stevens's own records, diaries, and correspondence about his work indicate only four possible encounters with Chief Seattle: a visit to the village of Seattle on an excursion around Puget Sound in January 1854; an emergency meeting there in March 1854, after violence between Indians and settlers on Whidbey Island; a possible but unrecorded meeting in December, shortly before the Port Elliott treaty council; and the Port Elliott council in January 1855.

Stevens's son, Hazard Stevens, surveyed his father's papers for a two-volume biography published in 1900. For the excursion Governor Stevens made around Puget Sound in January 1854, he quotes some records but admits that they are not as full as he could wish. He complains of the "provokingly brief and meagre record of this trip, which occupied the whole month of January" (Hazard Stevens, *Life*, 1:417). The governor traveled by a small sailboat in order (in his words) "to visit and take a census of the Indian tribes, learn something of the general character of the Sound and its harbors, and to visit Vancouver Island and its principal port, Victoria" (1:416). This trip therefore had at least three purposes. It was a preliminary survey of Indians in preparation for later treaty negotiations. It was a geographical excursion, to further Stevens's work in surveying a northern railway route. And it was a diplomatic mission, to look over the disputed boundaries between the United States and the British-held territories to the north. Stevens sailed up the eastern shoreline of Puget Sound and down the western shoreline, circling the disputed San Juan Islands.

His son quotes his report that he "saw a large body of Indians of nearly all the tribes [and] became greatly impressed with the important advantages of Seattle, and also with the importance of the disputed islands" (1:417). To the secretary of war the governor made particular mention of Seattle as the most advantageous port and the proper terminus of the transcontinental railroad. There is no mention of a meeting with Chief Seattle or an oration by any Indian (1:417), but Stevens somehow absorbed part of Seattle's message *before* he left on this first excursion. In a letter written to the commissioner of Indian affairs on December 26, 1853, just a month after his first arrival at the territorial capital, he described the Indians of Puget Sound as idle, sedentary people, who were prepared to sell their lands, except for a few reservations, to new settlers: "These spots are not only permanent places of residence, but are hereditary. Near them are the graves of their relatives and friends, and they cherish an affection for them which I have scarcely ever seen equalled" (Stevens, Letter, 6–7).

David Buerge has reasoned that this excursion is the most likely time for the meeting Smith has recorded. He dates the speech at January 12, 1854, in front of 1,200 Puget Sound Indians and 120 white settlers on the shore of Elliott Bay, the Seattle harborfront (Buerge, "Seattle's King Arthur," 28). The best evidence seems to be Smith's introduction to the speech in the *Star*: "When Governor Stevens first arrived in Seattle and told the natives he had been appointed commissioner of Indian affairs for Washington Territory, they gave him a demonstrative reception in front of Dr. Maynard's office, near the water front on Main street." Yet official records of this period, including other journals preserved in the National Archives, show no particular speech by Chief Seattle.[1]

Two months later, Stevens returned to Seattle suddenly, after Indians near Whidbey Island killed two white settlers (Richards, 196). Excited citizens at Seattle had sent a delegation to Olympia; the governor came in return, accompanied by a detachment of armed troops. On March 11 he held a formal, public meeting with Seattle and other chiefs, and he asked George Gibbs, one of his subordinates, to write up a full record of these proceedings. Many Indians and white citizens were present. A local settler translated from English into Chinook Jargon, and "an Indian translated as he went on" (Gibbs, "Notes," frame 0103, p. 2). This was a very important occasion for our purposes, for Governor Stevens chose this moment to name Seattle principal chief of Indians in the area and to declare that he would hold another chief and Seattle "responsible for the good behavior of their respective people, and would appoint subchiefs to support them in their authority." In other words, Stevens imposed the official identity of chief upon Seattle at this point, if not before; the report goes on to list the names of subchiefs that Seattle and the white officials agreed upon for the Duwamish and Suquamish tribes. Then, Gibbs reports, "after taking down the names Seattle made a great speech, declaring his good disposition toward the whites" (5). The other chief made a speech. Then Seattle related the Indian version of the crimes, which also involved murders of Indians by whites.

---

1. Rudolph Kaiser reports extensive searches made at the National Archives in 1983 (p. 533 *n8*). In 1985 a journal published by the National Archives featured an article about the speech citing several records of the period, but reporting no mention of an extended speech before the treaty councils of 1855 (Jerry L. Clark, 58–65).

There are no further details — no mention of the presence of Henry Smith or of a great gathering on the shores of Elliott Bay. Of course, it is likely that a great group gathered: the governor had come, there were sensational crimes to be dealt with, and (as Gibbs notes) there was suspicion of a concerted Indian uprising in the offing (6). The settler who translated English to Chinook Jargon came from a distance up the Duwamish River. David Maynard was surely present (he had led the delegation to Olympia) and Smith was very likely there.

This March meeting stands out as a tantalizing possibility for several reasons. It took place in public, in Seattle, with Chief Seattle and Governor Stevens addressing each other before a large public. Gibbs explicitly says that Seattle made "a great speech," though he gives no further details. Finally, the speech Henry Smith reports contains some notable passages about an end to violence. The speech apologizes for young warriors' rash acts of vengeance and hopes "that hostilities between the red-man and his pale-face brothers may never return." These points do not fit very well into a general speech about the exchange of lands for treaty benefits. They seem better suited to an occasion such as this, of peacemaking after a specific incident of bloodshed.

Yet this March 1854 occasion of peacemaking hardly suits Seattle's famous speech as a whole. It leaves little scope for a scene of stately leave-taking on Seattle's part. Instead the chief appears in Gibbs's record as a cooperative intermediary, defending the reports and actions of particular Indians and accepting his new role as an appointed official responsible to the governor. Besides, the issue to which every ear was tuned was violence between Indians and settlers, not land negotiations or a landscape hallowed by spirits of past generations.

Further light is shed on this meeting in the private journal that Gibbs kept and used in making his official report. As we will see in some detail, Gibbs was an ambiguous witness of Indians and their ways, urging harsh measures as matters of policy but making close observations out of a deep scientific curiosity. His journal pages for this period reveal that he was keenly interested in local mythology and supernatural practices and beliefs. If Seattle's "great speech" on this occasion was that recorded by Henry Smith, it seems odd that Gibbs failed to note its long passages about rival gods, persisting spirits, and *tahmanawis* beliefs. Gibbs must have been listening, for he reports that when Seattle ended his "great speech," he went on to explain many details of what he knew about the Whidbey murders.

Gibbs's journal contains several extensive notes on Puget Sound Indian beliefs in the supernatural. He records stories about encounters with stars that came down from the sky and begot children with two young women. He reports legends about haunted lakes. He describes a syncretic funeral ceremony, in which the corpse was dressed "in a suit of regimentals with a cocked hat and a pair of blue glass goggles and tied . . . upright on a white horse" and carried on a procession of twenty miles to his grave. He mentions the operations of "Skookum Sticks" and the death of a young Indian "from the effects of one of the tamahnous operations."[2] Later on, Gibbs consolidated his researches into a full account of Indian mythology, including a long section on *tahmanawis* beliefs and practices (Ella Clark, "George Gibbs' Account"). When he was at camp for the Port Elliott treaty council, he made a note for

---

2. Gibbs, Journal. The text is not paginated. I quote from my own microfilm copy; if the cover frame is taken as frame 001, these passages appear on frames 019–020, 022.

January 10: "In the evening went to see a Doctor in [amook?] tamanöus" (Gibbs, Journal, frame 042). In short, Gibbs seems to have been alert and persistent in tracing hints about Indian beliefs in general and *tahmanawis* practice in particular. In the 1850s he thought it a form of "mania"; he concludes the account of the Indian who died: "The circumstances and clear activities of this case as described, resemble perfectly those of Millerism, spirit rapping and others of perverted mental action from excitement" (frame 022).

Nonetheless, he went out of his way to collect fascinating stories and reports on precisely this subject. How then could he have missed a chief's extensive and explicit account of spiritual immanence — when it was spoken aloud and in public before him, and when he was particularly expected to keep good records?

The two further possibilities of an encounter between Stevens and Seattle are the months of December 1854 and January 1855. Stevens returned from his eastern trip late in the year and almost immediately addressed the territorial legislature and conducted other official business. He then set out to make a series of treaties with all the Indians west of the Cascade Mountains. He addressed the legislature on December 4, counseled with other officials, and began preparations for the first major treaty council, at Medicine Creek (on the Nisqually Flats between Olympia and Fort Steilacoom). Stevens arrived at the council ground on Christmas Eve and seems to have kept moving from one council to another for the next several weeks, returning to Olympia on February 6, 1855.

Rudolph Kaiser has proposed that some time in December Stevens went to Seattle: "The most likely date for the address seems to be December 1854, when Stevens returned from a trip to the East" (504). Kaiser's date, for which he provides no evidence or reasoning, contradicts Smith's statement that Stevens appeared soon after he first arrived as superintendent of Indian affairs. Stevens was an active man who could often accomplish much in a very short time. But his schedule was already crowded in December 1854, and it is hard to see what advantage he would have gained by meeting Chief Seattle separately just before or after a big council meeting at Medicine Creek. It is also odd that there is no record of such a public meeting about treaty proposals, at just the time when Stevens was conducting formal councils with formal records.

Again, George Gibbs's private journal provides a sidelight on this situation. Gibbs's entry for December 26 — on the council ground at Medicine Creek — records that it was just then, that late in the month, that Stevens decided "to call all the rest of Indians on the eastern shore into one council." The next day the various appointments for a series of Puget Sound treaty councils were made, with Gibbs as chief surveyor and acting secretary to the commission (Gibbs, Journal, frames 039–040). In other words, Stevens seems to have been far too busy with territorial duties on his first arrival to complete all the necessary arrangements for the treaty councils, let alone to project extra visits to meet with particular Indian leaders.

The Point Elliott council took place in late January. As he did for all the councils, Stevens arranged to have careful records kept of his major proposals and the replies made by Indian leaders. The records of Seattle's speeches on this occasion do not at all match the speech recorded by Smith. Besides, this was a meeting with Seattle and three other principal Indian leaders. It took place away from the city of Seattle, at a spot to the north now called Mukilteo. And Smith's account explicitly denies that this could have been the time and place. In his closing paragraph, Smith describes the reply of Governor Stevens: "He merely promised to meet them in general council on some future occasion to discuss the proposed treaty." Unless Smith's records or memory are very wrong, this general council, where the treaty was proposed and signed, must have occurred long after the time of Seattle's great speech.

Without Smith's account as a provocation for scrutinizing every line of every other record, there would be little to suggest that Chief Seattle once made a formal, noble oration to the governor at the waterfront on Elliott Bay. With Smith's account, the evidence seems to allow a slender possibility that some such address was made in January or March 1854.

But the full historical record raises many other problems about the speech. Other details about Seattle and Isaac Stevens stand out in the stories, meetings, and speeches around these records. The sharp, dramatic scene of a towering chief and an officious little governor is flattened out and compromised by ways they met and behaved on these and other occasions.

In the first place, Isaac Stevens emerges as a remarkably literate figure. He was a soldier trained at West Point and the disciplined surveyor of the northern railway route. He knew the value of keeping extensive and accurate records. He was, as well, an inveterate keeper of journals and a frequent correspondent. He jotted down the significant events of his life day after day after day, and often elaborated on them for his family and friends. That he did *not* record a speech by Chief Seattle is just as remarkable an omission as Gibbs's silence. Yet Stevens left no later anecdote, no hint of such a great oration. His son, who came along with him to many treaty councils, later surveyed all his papers — many years after Smith's account had been printed in 1887 and reprinted in

1891 — in order to publish his detailed biography. Hazard Stevens, too, notes no speech by Chief Seattle apart from the Port Elliott council.

Moreover, Stevens had a developed literary taste and a particular interest in oratorical performances. He was an ambitious student at West Point, who graduated at the top of his class — with specially commended talent in mathematics. But he was aware of the narrowness of his military training and worked hard to compensate. He read assiduously and sought out companions who would discuss books. At West Point he was valedictorian and founder of a literary magazine (Hazard Stevens, *Life*, 1:57); as a young officer he organized and participated in a lecture series (1:92). He made a point of going to hear congressional debates and supreme court arguments when he was in Washington, D.C. (1:75). While returning to Rhode Island from his sister's funeral, he stopped in Boston to hear John Quincy Adams's discourse on the four stages of human development, from savagery to civilization. Typically, he summarized the contents of Adams's address and commented on its style in a letter to his father (1:73). When he came to Washington Territory, he was authorized to develop a territorial library, and spent five thousand dollars, personally selecting the works of Addison, Swift, and Carlyle, and three hundred titles of history and biography. Thirty years after the end of his term few books had been added to this original collection (Richards, 172-73). Isaac Stevens, in short, may well have been the best prepared settler in the entire territory to hear and appreciate an extraordinary speech.

His accounts of particular Indian speeches are sometimes extensive. If he heard something striking, even something strikingly hostile, he was likely to make a note of it. Dozens of speeches are recorded in his papers and quoted in his son's biography. But his notes on Chief Seattle make no mention of particular oratorical power. His highest praise in that line goes to another, Spotted Eagle of the Nez Perce, who made a speech at a council in eastern Washington (September 17, 1856) "which for feeling, courage, and truth I have never seen surpassed in an Indian council" (2:219).

If Stevens emerges from the record as larger than Smith implies, Chief Seattle emerges as less. His other recorded speeches, his direct acquiescence at the treaty negotiations, and his past history all fall short of Smith's profile of a heroic defender of a deep Indian spirituality.

At Port Elliott, Seattle spoke twice according to official records. Both times he spoke briefly, just a paragraph or so on the page. Here is the dialogue recorded for January 22, 1855:

Gov. S. "Does any one object to what I have said? Does my venerable friend Seattle object? I want Seattle to give his will to me and to his people?["]

Seattle. "I look upon you as my father. I and the rest regard you as such. All of the Indians have the same good feeling toward you and will send it on paper to the Great Father. All of them[—]men, old men, women and children rejoice that he has sent you to take care of them. My mind is like yours. I don't want to say more. My heart is very good towards Dr. Maynard (a physician who was present) I want always to get medicine from him." (Documents . . . , roll 5, frame 0285; quoted in facsimile in Jerry L. Clark, "Thus Spoke Chief Seattle")

This is not stalwart dignity but abject submission. The last lines play right into Stevens's hands. He immediately promised that the Indians would have a doctor to look after them. He then asked for (and got) three cheers to ratify Seattle's agreement — and turned to Patkenim, chief of the Snohomish, to secure an expression of his goodwill, too.

The next day, January 23, after Stevens distributed a few presents,

> *Seattle* then on behalf of himself and the other Chiefs brought a white flag and presented it, saying: "Now by this we make friends and put away all bad feelings if we ever had any. We are the friends of the Americans. All the Indians are of the same mind. We look upon you as our Father. We will never change our minds, but since you have been to see us we will always be the same. Now! Now do you send this paper of our hearts to the Great Chief. That is all I have to say." (Documents . . . , p. 11, roll 5, frame 0287).

It may be objected that these records are the official records kept by Stevens and his agents. They were never read or reviewed by Seattle or any literate advocate on his behalf. But the records of other councils record angry words by leaders who were offended by Stevens's proposals, some of whom refused to sign. Some bargained for better advantages. Some signed but later led uprisings against white settlements. The record shows that Seattle agreed to what was offered, led the others in signing, quietly accepted the treaty, and respected its terms. During Indian wars that followed a year after Stevens's tour of treaty-making, Seattle remained notably friendly even to the point of sending warnings to the settlements when he learned of plans for surprise attacks. Smith's account concludes: "Chief Seattle's promise to adhere to the treaty, should one be ratified, was observed to the letter, for he was ever the unswerving and faithful friend of the white man." On this point all the early authorities agree.

David Buerge has called attention to a speech recorded in 1850 by Benjamin F. Shaw, who later served as Stevens's interpreter during the treaty councils. Shaw and his party came upon a group of Indians on the east shore of Elliott Bay on the sand spit where the city of Seattle was established a few years later. These Indians came rushing down to the shore, shaking knives and blankets and shooting guns. A large man then spoke to the intruders, through another Indian who spoke Chinook Jargon:

> My name is Sealt, and this great swarm of people that you see here are my people; they have come down here to celebrate the coming of the first run of good salmon. As the salmon are our chief food we always rejoice to see them coming early and in abundance, for that insures us a plentiful quantity of food for the coming winter. This is the reason our hearts are glad today, and so you do not want to take this wild demonstration as warlike. It is meant in the nature of a salute in imitation of the Hudson Bay Company's salute to their chiefs when they arrive at Victoria. I am glad to have you come to our country, for we Indians know but little and you Boston and King George men [know] how to do everything. We want your blankets, your guns, axes, clothing and tobacco, and all other things that you make. We need all these things that you make, as we do not know how to make them, and so we welcome you to our country to make flour, sugar and other things that we can trade for. We wonder why the Boston men should wander so far away from their home and come among so many Indians. Why are you not afraid?[3]

---

3. Buerge, "The Man We Call Seattle," 25. In a recent souvenir booklet, *Chief Seattle*, Buerge ascribes this passage to the Clarence B. Bagley Manuscript Collection, special collections, University of Washington. In fact, the Bagley Collection does not include such a manuscript. This speech is preserved in what appears to be the carbon copy of Bagley's draft typescript of an unpublished article on this incident: Clarence B. Bagley papers, box 18, file 16. I quote from this source, silently correcting obvious typing errors.

Obviously this is not the transcription of a speech but a summary of many disjointed remarks taken down through a cumbersome process of translation. But it coincides in interesting ways with the Smith report — in referring to "King George men" and expressing puzzlement that Americans would travel so far from their homes. This whole incident also seems to shed new light on these original inhabitants. Shaw and his party walked up the beach "to the high ground where a long, low shed of a house stood; it was built of split cedar boards and was about two hundred feet long by 40 feet wide. In the interior of the house were long rows of bunks, which lined each side of the building, and a large space was left open in the middle in which fires were kept burning by the families for cooking purposes." These descriptions match the general pattern of Puget Sound Indian housing at this time. They also indicate a settled habitation on the Elliott Bay waterfront, which was displaced and eradicated when white settlers platted their claims.

This encounter ended with a "Tomanawous" ceremony (as this record spells it) witnessed by Shaw and his party: the initiation of a medicine man, who returned from a sacred encounter in the woods and came "rolling and tumbling, snapping and biting and frothing at the mouth" until he plunged into the bay "where he stood biting pieces of his flesh out of his own body and swallowing them."

Evidently Shaw's record is a letter or report written at least a few years after this visit to Elliott Bay, for it closes, "Thus ended my first reception in Seattle." Seattle was not named Seattle until 1852. It is therefore hard to know how much to credit the details here. The speech that Shaw here ascribes to "Sealt" cannot be a verbatim report, nor can Shaw's elaborate reply about the force and prosperity of the coming hordes of white settlers. But Sealt's speech, in general, implies a friendly submissiveness on the part of his people. They are already on good terms with other traders, already eager for trade goods. They seem to move all over Puget Sound — at least as far as Victoria — and to be already dependent on the invaders ("men who know how to do everything") for many necessities.

Despite Shaw's report of a "Tomanawous" ceremony, Seattle's early compromise with white invaders extended even into his spiritual life. He had been converted to Christianity by Jesuit missionaries many years earlier and he remained a Catholic of sorts. At his death in 1866 he was buried after "funeral services of the Roman Catholic Church," according to an extensive account published a few years later (Scammon, 299; rpt. in *Seattle Post Intelligencer*, Jan. 1, 1884, Bagley, *History*, 1:79–80). Governor Stevens could appeal to a common Christianity when he addressed the Indians at Port Elliott. "I find that many of you are Christians, and I saw among you yesterday the sign of the Cross, which I think the most holy of all signs. I address you therefore mainly as Christians, who know that this life is a preparation for the life to come. You want not simply a home on this Earth, where you and your children will be cared for, but you want a home for the next world" (Document . . . , p. 4, roll 5, frame 0280). Later, before the treaty was read, "the Indians sung a Mass, after the Roman Catholic Form, and recited a prayer" (p. 8, roll 5, frame 0284).

Probably Seattle observed and balanced some Christian rituals with traditional tribal beliefs and practices. But he could not have been a spokesman for Indian spirituality unalloyed. Smith reports his making a long attack on white men's religion and claiming that his beliefs were quite different. But how much of this passage is believable as the voice of even a loosely practicing Roman Catholic?

Your God loves your people and hates mine; he folds his strong arms lovingly around the white man and leads him as a father leads his infant son, but he has forsaken his red children; he makes your people wax strong every day, and soon they will fill the land; while my people are ebbing away like a fast-receding tide, that will never flow again. The white men's God cannot love his red children or he would protect them. They seem to be orphans and can look nowhere for help. How then can we become brothers? How can your father become our father and bring us prosperity and awaken in us dreams of returning greatness?

Your God seems to us to be partial. He came to the white man. We never saw Him; never even heard His voice; He gave the white man laws but He had no word for His red children whose teeming millions filled this vast continent as the stars fill the firmament. No, we are two distinct races and must ever remain so. There is little in common between us. . . .

Your religion was written on tables of stone by the iron finger of an angry God, lest you might forget it. The red man could never remember nor comprehend it.

Our religion is the traditions of our ancestors, the dreams of our old men, given them by the great Spirit, and the visions of our sachems, and is written in the hearts of our people.

There may be a flash of momentary anger or frustration here. There may be recollections of some biblical imagery. But the stress on one god for "them" and another for "us," with "little in common between us," just does not ring true to the friendly, Christian Chief Seattle of other pioneer recollections.[4] Nor does it

---

4. A diary from 1854 describes an Indian Catholic Mass celebrated near Steilacoom in Chinook Jargon and a local Indian language, with the aid of parchment rolls covered with pictures (McDonald, "Hard Work").

match his peoples' Christian practices, in his time and after.

Smith's account of the setting of the speech must also be read very carefully. "When Governor Stevens first arrived in Seattle and told the natives he had been appointed commissioner of Indian affairs for Washington Territory, they gave him a demonstrative reception in front of Dr. Maynard's office, near the water front on Main street." This sentence need not imply a large settled community with many streets and many buildings, including a doctor's office. Such imagery does not square very well with a date in 1854 or 1855. The first white settlements in what is now Seattle began in the Duwamish River valley and at Alki on the western shore outside Elliott Bay late in 1851. The village on Elliott Bay began to take shape after April 1852. In fact, Chief Seattle had led a party down to Olympia to encourage Dr. David Maynard to bring his failing dry goods business up to a better trading point, where there were also plenty of fish to be pickled for shipment to California. In a friendly return, it was probably Maynard who proposed naming the place Seattle.[5] When Henry A. Smith first arrived that same spring, he could hardly find the place: "There were a few

George Gibbs notes that when Skagit Indians arrived at Port Elliott on January 12, "the men filed off & walked up towards the camp of the Snoqualmoos & the latter in like manner marched down, passing one another they saluted with the sign of the cross, taking off their hatts & then countermarching broke into knots & exchanged news with one another. The whole was done with great ceremony & respect." After dark there was a "'divine service' in their camp singing and preaching" (Gibbs, Journal, frame 042).

5. Grant, 71; Bagley, *History*, 1:21, and "Chief Seattle and Angeline," 245. Both historians repeat the story that Seattle was (at least at first) uncomfortable at having his name used for a settlement because he feared his spirit would be called and disturbed after his death.

cabins at that time, but they were so hidden by the immense timber that the shore appeared practically a wilderness. Coming along in a canoe with Collins [another settler], he asked where the town was, for there was nothing visible from the shore except for a small improvement of Dr. Maynard's" (Grant, 86), In what became another famous story, Smith himself was bewildered by the tall timber: "In the course of his work of settlement he started out one day to blaze a trail from the cove which still bears his name to the Village of Seattle, became lost without knowing it and described a huge circle which brought him to his own back fence. Here he sat for some time and reflected on the similarity between this strange clearing and his own" (Bagley, *History*, 1:26). Henry Yesler arrived later in 1852 and set up a sawmill on the waterfront, with a cookhouse and a general hall. The town soon drew its income by trading timber and pilings to San Francisco. Maynard had a small store where he lived and traded goods with Indians and immigrants. He also practiced medicine; served as a justice of the peace, notary, and local Indian agent; and slowly went broke with improvident generosity and ill-planned land schemes.[6] It would be decades before this village had more than a few thousand inhabitants. In 1854 it held a few dozen, mainly in rough wooden buildings on streets unpaved. Early maps and sketches show a few cabins along the shore and out onto an eight-acre point.[7]

There were only a few thousand white settlers in all of western Washington by 1854. Chief Seattle had certainly seen Olympia, the capital, and Victoria at the other end of Puget Sound. But his

---

6. Bagley, *History*, 1:20–27. For the color and detail of early Seattle and Doc Maynard's place in it, see also Morgan, 11–57.

7. Bagley, *History*, 1:21; a very helpful diagram and map appear in LeWarne, 120.

words about "cities" later in his famous speech can refer to nothing like a city as we know it: "At night, when the streets of your cities and villages shall be silent, and you think them deserted, they will throng with the returning hosts that once filled and still love this beautiful land." Those throngs and hosts are also cumulative — the *generations* of Indians who passed over the lands and fished the waters.

One final touch worth mentioning is that if Governor Stevens arrived and announced his appointment as superintendent of Indian affairs, he probably did not stand on ceremony, despite all his titles. He was a short man with a large head, and he was known to dress in rough clothing when he went out to new settlements. On Christmas Day 1854, at the Medicine Creek treaty council, he was dressed "in a red flannel shirt with his pants tucked into the boots 'California style,' but as a concession to the Indians, who preferred that important people dress the part, he wore a dark frock coat and black felt hat with a clay pipe stuck in the band" (Richards, 199).

Governor Stevens's arrival and official pronouncements matched other recent changes in the scene around Elliott Bay. In 1853, an act of Congress had created Washington Territory by separating the region north of the Columbia River from Oregon, and setting the eastern boundary at the Continental Divide. And for the village just developing out of a few land plots and a sawmill, a new name went into the records. On May 23, 1853, "Seattle" became the official name and spelling of the place (Bagley, *History*, 1:27) and, by extension, the official treaty name of the Indian who lived nearby.

This may be the most crucial point of all about Chief Seattle's speech. The speech claims to speak for a people who have inhabited and cherished the region and to speak for the land itself — the beautiful land that will always hold watchful guardian spirits from a long past. The voice of Chief Seattle appropriately speaks to and for the history of the place called Seattle. But the transfer of identity between this man and the land also works the other way. Once the village was named Seattle, the man also became a personification of the place. Not quite an eponymous founder, nor a human mascot, this single Indian became "Chief Seattle" because it was convenient for the new settlers' laws and policies. Land claims, treaty making, and treaty enforcement required a single person to represent a whole people and their claims to a wide territory. Whatever the name he may have had before, whatever the ranking or authority he may have held among his own people, he was "chief" and "Seattle" indelibly after 1853.[8]

His mark on the treaty, his neutrality and support to settlers during the subsequent Indian wars, and his death in 1866 all permitted the rise of an ever larger settlement. He could hover at a safe distance — at the reservation on the other side of Puget Sound and soon in his grave there — as a respectable, benignant spirit. If there was a touch of melancholy attached to his memory and his displacement, that mood also fitted with early settlers' own hard-

---

8. There are still arguments over the correct spelling or pronunciation of Seattle's original name. Another common version is Sealth. But names are a tricky business, especially when transliterated from one language to another. If I may cite a homely but very pertinent example: My mother's name is spelled Lourice and usually I have heard it as a rhyme for *chorus*. But her mother, who named her, called her by one syllable — Larse; her older brother called her Lorse; some neighbors and co-workers put an accent on the second syllable, so that her name rhymed with *police*. She answered to all those names, and I never heard her suggest a correction.

ships and their own sense of loss when others arrived and began to displace them.

David Buerge explains the appearance of Smith's article in 1887 as, in part, an admonition from one generation of these later settlers to another:

> In 1887, Henry Smith was 57, about a decade younger than Chief Seattle had been at the time of the speech. Smith and his pioneer compatriots had done very well in the meantime. They had become middle-class landowners, a propertied elite that liked to call itself "Old Seattle." They had run the town for decades, but by the mid 1880s they were losing power to a growing working class and to a class of urbane professionals and entrepreneurs who styled themselves as "New Seattle."
>
> The competition between these groups heated up in the mid-'80s, and tensions between the middle and working classes erupted into violence, culminating in the anti-Chinese riots of 1885-1886. In the municipal elections of 1886, radical populists came to power, and there was talk of revolution and of doing away with the propertied elite, referred to sneeringly as "dog-salmon aristocrats." The anger and fear was very real, and Smith and his pioneer colleagues felt themselves to be in much the same situation as the one they had put the Indians in in the 1850s. (Buerge, "Seattle's King Arthur," 28–29)

It was in response to this situation that Smith wrote his series of pioneer reminiscences for the *Star*. The article about Chief Seattle was the tenth installment. "It was a vivid way of saying that those who do not remember history are condemned to repeat it" (29).

We can now see that in the course of meeting that local crisis of the 1880s, Smith also composed a rich legend for his century.

The face-to-face confrontation of an articulate Indian with a government agent is one thing. But a spiritual Indian facing the man who had just mapped the transcontinental railroad route! There is a mural for the whole American nineteenth century and a wonderful symbol for the founding of a great city.

Other American cities have Indian names: Manhattan, Chicago, Omaha. Indian names cover the map in Washington State. Some American cities commemorate great American leaders: Washington, Jefferson, Jackson, Lincoln. On the West Coast some of the major ports commemorate saints and angels. But by Smith's account, Seattle is named for an Indian leader who was also a spiritual guide, who performed his greatest act at the time of modern settlement. The settlers' original name for their spot was New York–Alki. (In Chinook Jargon, *alki* means "by and by" or "in a while.") But when they found a better location across the bay, they adopted a name that fitted both their new home and the people they dispossessed. And that name has come to have its own power. As a child of Seattle I can bear witness that the sight of that name or an analogous word on a sign or on a screen — "seal," "seat," "settle," "satellite," "stealth" — can still make me come alert with recognition, like overhearing my own name in a company of strangers.

Yet the evidence of how Seattle became a "chief" as well as a city as well as a spokesman for spiritual mysteries is riddled with every likelihood of cultural ventriloquism. Even if Henry Smith's remaining tattered page points to some actual utterance he took notes on, on the spot, it remains misleading, for it reshapes an event in modern terms. And the event itself was already determined and prepared by Europeans and Americans from the East Coast. They had long since brought trade goods, religion, an intermediate jargon, promises, and threats, to make over Indians in their own image. They had already assimilated Seattle — in name if not in person — before any governor needed to arrive and engage in formal treaties or formal addresses.

AMERICA'S REPLY

CHAPTER 4

Answers from Afar

THE SPEECH OF CHIEF SEATTLE must, by now, seem barely credible as an event in history. Corruptions of text, extravagances of language, distortions of translation, and inconsistencies of meaning all stand in the way of our hearing Seattle's voice. Conflicting records and the outlines of myth stand between us and any possible date and place where that voice might have spoken.

And yet the mythic pressure of this speech endures and will endure. Perhaps rightly so. The person who led the Duwamish and Suquamish people has left just a few traces in the historical record. But in his place there remains a legendary figure, a symbol partly created and much enlarged by white men: a "Chief Seattle" officially named by Governor Stevens, and a "sable old orator" reported by Henry Smith and reshaped by later editors. In return for the distortions of white invaders and those who come after them, this figure goes on unceasingly in his reproaches. Looked at squarely, his message in its earliest traceable form is not a testament about ecology or pristine, uninhabited nature. It is rather an expression of mingled pride and sorrow about long habitation in a beautiful region. As he relinquishes his claims to much of the Puget Sound territory, Seattle admonishes the new settlers. He recalls the generations that have dwelled there, to whom every feature in the landscape has had meaning and been precious. He notes that past generations have died and been absorbed into the soil. But their spirits cannot leave their home. They will remain there to the end of time, revisiting those scenes. Seattle's long closing passage dwells on these ideas:

Every part of this country is sacred to my people. Every hill-side, every valley, every plain and grove has been hallowed by some fond memory or some sad experience of my tribe. Even the rocks that seem to lie dumb as they swelter in the sun along the silent sea-shore in solemn grandeur thrill with memories of past events connected with the fate of my people, and the very dust under your feet responds more lovingly to our footsteps than to yours, because it is the ashes of our ancestors, and our bare feet are conscious of the sympathetic touch, for the soil is rich with the life of our kindred.

The sable braves, and fond mothers, and glad-hearted maidens, and the little children who lived and rejoiced here and whose very names are now forgotten, still love these solitudes, and their deep fastnesses at eventide grow shadowy with the presence of dusky spirits. And when the last red man shall have perished from the earth and his memory among white men shall have become a myth, these shores shall swarm with the invisible dead of my tribe, and when your children's children shall think themselves alone in the field, the store, the shop, upon the highway or in the silence of the woods they will not be alone. . . . At night, when the streets of your cities and villages shall be silent, and you think them deserted, they will throng with the returning hosts that once filled and still love this beautiful land. The white man will never be alone. Let him be just and deal kindly with my people, for the dead are not altogether powerless.

There are analogous appeals in other speeches by Indians, including leaders who met in treaty councils with Governor Stevens. Many objected to leaving familiar places and ancestral burial grounds. But there is no speech quite so sustained on this theme, and none expresses the same point about permanent spirits dwelling in the relinquished lands. Are these Henry Smith's ideas, projected onto a figure from the past? Are they a haunting idea Smith absorbed from local Indians or from one or many speeches around Puget Sound? Whatever their origin, these ideas, embodied in this now-famous speech, address a deep-running problem of more than local interest. Who does own the American landscape? What peoples have dwelled upon it most harmoniously or wisely? How has the vast invasion from Europe since the sixteenth century been absorbed by the North American continent? How has this land impressed itself back upon the progeny and successors of its invaders? And how can peoples who have now come together here over generations, from every continent around the globe, dwell with a sense of belonging?

The speech does not answer these questions, but it certainly raises them. We have looked with searching scrutiny at its text and historical setting, until nothing but questions remains. But the questions are as powerful as they come.

If we regard the speech — whatever its origins — as a painful voicing of these questions, then the critical problem to be addressed is not just its source but how it can be heard and answered. And to take the speech on its own terms, we need to look to the wider setting of America in the 1850s. How, we must ask, could a figure like Governor Stevens have taken it in, even if he did not leave any record of it? How could Dr. Henry Smith, or others in the early village of Seattle? How could a representative, literate, informed listener from the eastern United States have paid attention to such an utterance? Into what framework of thinking could he have accommodated it?

Three well-known writers of early America provide some suggestive answers: Thomas Jefferson, Walt Whitman, and Nathaniel Hawthorne. Some of their most famous works include telling passages about Indians or the inhabiting of American land; they can serve as typical and very articulate examples of three different but very pertinent mental outlooks.

Jefferson's thinking is perhaps the closest to that of Stevens, especially in his official capacities as governor and treaty maker. Jefferson pays close attention to Indian oratory; he also questions the place of Indians and Europeans in the politics, geography, and resources of North America. But in the end, he keeps his official distance. Jefferson is a reader of such extensive learning that he diminishes an Indian to a specimen in a vast collection; he assimilates Indian oratory into his library, his domain of literate power. We might call this attitude an Attentive Official Deafness. That phrase makes a peculiar oxymoron around "official," but it fits the deep paradox of American curiosity about Indians, combined with a numbed incapacity to recognize their full humanity.

Whitman seems to pay attention very differently, overturning libraries with a sweep of his arm in the name of revitalizing a voice, an authentic, powerful, indigenous American singing voice. But he, too, assimilates Indian voices. He blends them and others into a vast new and individual American breath and personally claims to embrace all people in all regions of this continent. It is worth noticing that Whitman was composing and printing off his first copies of *Leaves of Grass* in the mid-1850s, just when Isaac Stevens was making his treaties with the Indians of Washington Territory.

Finally, from about this time, we have a different personal voice in the pages of *The Scarlet Letter*. In its opening section, Hawthorne makes a curious and perplexed meditation about the life of a family or tribe so long in one American place that ghosts haunt descendents and hold them trapped and doomed. Against such a pressure from the past, Hawthorne replies with an emphatic protest.

These figures thus represent tellingly different attitudes — Jefferson, the official, learned, and distant; Whitman, the aggressively, personally assimilative; and Hawthorne, the awkwardly and painfully dynastic. These are not only individual moods. In a sense they are three aspects of a developed patriotism in the eastern United States. We can find them repeated and varied in other writers and thinkers of this period; we shall meet all of them again, in fact, when we discuss Governor Stevens in detail. But for now they deserve analysis in these distinct and famous voices. For these three writers urge separate American answers to Chief Seattle, even though none of them could have heard or read his speech. Their writings anticipate a voice like Seattle's and shape the kind of listening others could have offered on the shores of Puget Sound.

It is largely through Thomas Jefferson's acts as a statesman that Americans came to dwell in the Pacific Northwest. He guided and administered the complicated negotiations known as the Louisiana Purchase, which annexed lands west of the Mississippi to the United States. He shaped important laws about federal lands, the ordinances by which regions could become territories and eventually achieve admission to full statehood. And as a diligent reader and student in many branches of learning, he tried to understand the full dimensions of North America. He mastered an extensive library about its geography, climate, plants, animals, and peoples. He read about the most recent explorations and fostered new ones. Most notably he initiated, sponsored, and directed the Lewis and Clark expedition of 1803–1806. This was the first party of American citizens to reach the headwaters of the Missouri, cross the Rockies, and descend the Columbia River, thus laying legal and intellectual claim to the northern tier of the present United States. When Isaac Stevens went to Olympia as territorial governor, Indian negotiator, and surveyor of a northern railway route, he traveled almost fifty years after Lewis and Clark, but he followed maps and guidelines derived from Thomas Jefferson. Stevens was aware of that fact, and proud of it. In many of their attitudes toward the Far West, as we will see in the next chapter, Stevens and Jefferson were of the same mind.

Not all of Jefferson's complicated and sometimes contradictory ideas about the West and Indian policies need detain us here. For our purposes, we can focus on just one celebrated incident, his defense of Indian oratory in *Notes on the State of Virginia*. His terms are those of a scholar, a person of extensive reading, who stands far removed from any danger of being affected by oratory alone. He frames a great Indian speech within well-worn categories of literate expectation, and so ignores even its most patent appeal.

Jefferson's terms of praise are famous and extravagant: "I may challenge the whole orations of Demosthenes and Cicero, and of any more eminent orator, if Europe has furnished more eminent, to produce a single passage superior to the speech of Logan, a Mingo Chief, to Lord Dunmore, when governor of this state" (Jefferson, 62). He explains that Logan's speech arose from controversies between Indians and "land-adventurers" in western lands along the Ohio River. In 1774 some Indians committed robbery, and the whites retaliated with raids. They murdered women and children, including all of Logan's family. In Jefferson's words:

> Among these were unfortunately the family of Logan, a chief celebrated in peace and war, and long distinguished as the friend of the whites. This unworthy return provoked his vengeance. He accordingly signalized himself in the war which ensued. In the autumn of the same year a decisive battle was fought at the mouth of the Great Kanhaway, between the collected forces of the

Shawanese, Mingoes, and Delawares, and a detachment of the Virginia militia. The Indians were defeated, and sued for peace. Logan however disdained to be seen among the suppliants. But, lest the sincerity of a treaty should be distrusted, from which so distinguished a chief absented himself, he sent by a messenger the following speech to be delivered to Lord Dunmore.[1]

The printed speech is of course a translation. But it was originally made by a fortuitous agent — General John Gibson, who was both Logan's brother-in-law and Lord Dunmore's envoy to the treaty conference (300 *n 3*). Jefferson notes that the speech was immediately repeated around Williamsburg, copied in newspapers all over the colonies and in Great Britain, and set as a memorization exercise in colonial schools (227). In citing the speech he invokes not only the force of one speaker but a fame enlarged by repetition in white settlements, printed newspapers, and schoolbooks.

Here, from Jefferson's account, is Logan's speech:

> I appeal to any white man to say, if ever he entered Logan's cabin hungry, and he gave him not meat; if ever he came cold and naked, and he clothed him not. During the course of the last long and bloody war, Logan remained idle in his cabin, an advocate for peace. Such was my love for the whites, that my countrymen pointed as they passed, and said, "Logan is the friend of white men." I had even thought to have lived with you, but for the injuries of one man. Col. Cresap, the last spring, in cold blood, and unprovoked, murdered all the relations of Logan, not sparing even my

---

1. Jefferson, 62–63. This account is a revised version, which Jefferson penned after seeking and reviewing many documents about this case. Editor William Peden notes that Jefferson's original version, attacking Col. Michael Cresap for the murders of Logan's family, involved Jefferson in protracted controversies (ibid., 298–300).

women and children. There runs not a drop of my blood in the veins of any living creature. This called on me for revenge. I have sought it: I have killed many: I have fully glutted my vengeance. For my country, I rejoice at the beams of peace. But do not harbour a thought that mine is the joy of fear. Logan never felt fear. He will not turn on his heel to save his life. Who is there to mourn for Logan? — Not one. (Jefferson, 63)

As a performance, this is not unlike Chief Seattle's address. Again we have a sole spokesman addressing invaders and yielding to their invasion. Here, too, the Indian professes his longstanding friendship, then makes a melancholy close. Again there is the last flicker of noble resistance, but against an impending threat of black annihilation. Henry Smith seems to have caught some of these similarities in his poem about the name Seattle:

> For a name sometimes turns to a slogan,
>> And stands as a symbol of right,
> As once did the name of great Logan,
>> That led in the van of the fight.

There is even the mordant irony that a meeting of beliefs has gone awry. The opening lines here recall a Gospel passage familiar to churchgoers of Jefferson's era:

When the Son of man shall come in his glory, and all the holy angels with him, then shall he sit upon the throne of his glory: and before him shall be gathered all nations: and he shall separate them one from another, as a shepherd divideth his sheep from the goats: and he shall set the sheep on his right hand, but the goats on the left. Then shall the King say unto them on his right hand, "Come, ye blessed of my Father, inherit the kingdom prepared for

you from the foundation of the world: for I was an hungred, and ye
gave me meat: I was thirsty, and ye gave me drink: I was a stranger
and ye took me in: naked, and ye clothed me." (Matthew 25:31–36,
King James version)

Logan's allusion implies at the very least that he has behaved with
every kind of Christian charity and been sorely punished for it.
But it could be more keenly devastating: at the Last Judgment,
Logan will be the blessed heir of a kingdom; when all nations are
gathered, his current tormenters will be the ones judged and
found wanting. In either case, this speech, like Seattle's, invokes
supernatural judgment in a conflict between peoples.

But if Jefferson ever heard these possibilities in Logan's speech
he does not say so. His treatment of it is what matters here, and
the way he places it in his writings shows that he is deaf to much
of what it says. We saw earlier that many transcriptions of Indian
speeches are shaped for literate audiences, so that one or two
main ideas are stressed. The Indians' expressions of outrage or
pain are safely insulated. Here the main message Logan sends to
Dunmore is that he accepts a treaty even though he will not sign
it. Another safe though affecting point is that he proclaims himself and his people to be on the verge of extinction. A third is that
Logan has been dangerous but is no longer: "I have fully glutted
my vengeance." A reader must search in order to bring out other
possibilities. In the speech's full context, in *Notes on the State of
Virginia*, Jefferson offers many wider frameworks of judgment,
such as that this speech is a specimen of oratory to be judged
against the works of Cicero or Demosthenes. Jefferson need not
mention that these were also speakers on the losing side of great
conflicts of empire. He expects his audience to understand that
oratory is a noble but ineffectual art.

He drives this point home in the paragraph that immediately follows the speech:

> Before we condemn the Indians of this continent as wanting ge-
> nius, we must consider that letters have not yet been introduced
> among them. Were we to compare them in their present state with
> the Europeans North of the Alps, when the Roman arms and arts
> first crossed those mountains, the comparison would be unequal,
> because, at that time, those parts of Europe were swarming with
> numbers; because numbers produce emulation, and multiply the
> chances of improvement, and one improvement begets another.
> Yet I may safely ask, How many good poets, how many able math-
> ematicians, how many great inventors in arts or sciences, had Eu-
> rope North of the Alps then produced? And it was sixteen centu-
> ries after this before a Newton could be formed. I do not mean to
> deny, that there are varieties in the race of man, distinguished by
> their powers both of body and mind. I believe there are, as I see to
> be the case in the races of other animals. (Jefferson, 63)

There seem to be different orders of human beings, and Indians are low among those orders — lower than the Teutons because less numerous, and therefore less likely to emulate each other and "multiply the chances of improvement." The Teutons in turn are lower than the Romans with their "arms and arts." And the Romans are at least sixteen centuries behind modern arts and sciences. As Jefferson and his correspondents understood the world, literacy and science rightly gave some people empire or dominion over others.

Jefferson explicitly denies that Indians have such power: "Letters have not yet been introduced among them." This point is historically incorrect, but it is good evidence of Jefferson's attitudes. Very specifically it means that he cannot have heard

Logan's allusion to the Bible, and certainly cannot have imagined such an Indian being subtle enough to turn a Gospel teaching back upon his teachers. Jefferson wants to draw the conclusion that Indians are *capable* of becoming fully human once they become fully civilized. But that may take centuries — and meanwhile whole tribes are becoming extinct.

In *Notes on the State of Virginia*, Logan's speech also fits into Jefferson's argument as a specimen among ranges of collected specimens. The book is organized as a compendium of answers Jefferson made as governor of Virginia to a series of questions posed in 1780 by the secretary of the French legation at Philadelphia. The answers to this questionnaire were delayed and interrupted by events of the Revolutionary War and Jefferson's personal life, and the project grew to be a book in the course of time. But it retains two important features because of these beginnings. It is a report by one public official to another, and a scientific survey of America, addressed to the learned minds of Europe.

The chapter that reports Logan's speech is titled "Productions Mineral, Vegetable and Animal." It is in this section that Jefferson directly faces and refutes the French naturalist Georges Louis Leclerc, compte de Buffon, who had published the charge that animals of the New World were smaller, fewer in species, and even degenerate in comparison to the animals in the Old (Jefferson, 47). Jefferson makes comparative lists of quadrupeds native to either Europe or America. He matches New World mammoths, bears, caribou, elk, and bison against any Old World deer, boars, and sheep that Buffon can name. He then moves on to consider human beings, quoting Buffon's charges that the indigenous North American is feeble, sexually dull, weak in mind as well as body, and lacking any ardor or strong emotional tie to mate, family, or society (58–59). Jefferson attacks all these charges. The account of Logan concludes this stage of the argument.

Jefferson defends Indians scientifically, treating them as a kind of superior social animal, which moves in hunting parties through hazardous territories, and therefore is less productive of offspring: "Even at their homes the nation depends for food, through a certain part of the year, on the gleanings of the forest: that is, they experience a famine once in every year. With all animals, if the female be badly fed, or not fed at all, her young perish: and if both male and female be reduced to like want, generation becomes less active, less productive" (60–61). Jefferson concludes with an estimate of Indians' mental powers: "To form a just estimate of their genius and mental powers, more facts are wanting, and great allowance to be made for those circumstances of their situation which call for a display of particular talents only. This done, we shall probably find that they are formed in mind as well as body, on the same module with the 'Homo sapiens Europaeus'" (62). In general, Jefferson believes that Indians can live very well without thinking. He explains on a later page that they live by a highly developed "moral sense," which takes the place of laws, government, and coercion. He idealizes his "savages" as in this sense superior to civilized people.[2] Jefferson explains the kinds of mental activity that Indians do exercise in very narrow terms. It all comes down to occasional displays of personal power — in war or, less frequently, in oratory.

---

2. "Were it made a question, whether no law, as among the savage Americans, or too much law, as among the civilized Europeans, submits man to the greatest evil, one who has seen both conditions would pronounce it the be the last: and that the sheep are happier of themselves, than under care of the wolves. It will be said, that great societies cannot exist without government. The Savages therefore break them into small ones" (Jefferson, 93).

The principles of their society forbidding all compulsion, they are
to be led to duty and to enterprize by personal influence and per-
suasion. Hence eloquence in council, bravery and address in war,
become the foundations of all consequence with them. To these
acquirements all their faculties are directed. Of their bravery and
address in war we have multiplied proofs, because we have been
the subjects on which they were exercised. Of their eminence in
oratory we have fewer examples, because it is displayed chiefly in
their own councils. Some, however, we have of very superior lustre.
I may challenge the whole orations of Demosthenes and Cicero,
and of any more eminent orator, if Europe has furnished more eminent, to produce a single passage, superior to the speech of Logan,
a Mingo chief, to Lord Dunmore, when governor of this state. (62)

In Jefferson's large design, therefore, the importance of Logan's
speech is very narrowly circumscribed. It is a rare example of illiterate reasoning power, used in place of direct military prowess, by
a person better led by other instincts. In a broader view, it fits into
a tour-de-force display of New World phenomena against Old
World misconceptions — with Indians ranked among animals,
vegetables, and minerals.

To return to Seattle and Governor Stevens: Jefferson's passage
reveals that even at his most enlightened, the Great White Father
in Washington was incapable of hearing any depth in a speech like
Seattle's — not even when he was listening! Of all the nineteenth-
century presidents, Jefferson was easily the most likely to pay attention to indigenous people and try to learn from them, just as
he and Lincoln were the most idealistic in defending human
equality. But if a speech like Seattle's had been transmitted even to
him, his response might have been only blank incomprehension.
When struck by the very similar lines of Logan's address, he could
not hear what it said. "Nothing Jefferson ever wrote," says his edi-

tor, "has evoked more controversy than the passage and its revision on the murder of Logan's family" (Jefferson, 298 *n 1*). Jefferson sought out and weighed many further accounts *about* Logan and the *circumstances* of his message. But he seems never to have reconsidered the power of the speech itself.

Worse yet, his behavior here is an object lesson about the inherent prejudices of the highly literate. Jefferson evidently admired Logan's speech. He must have copied it with his own hand, word for word, and preserved it for many years. But to impart it to other readers he had to place it in some category of shared, literate learning. And to categorize was to subordinate it within frame upon frame, until what began as striking speech was choked off and squeezed between heavy books to become an obscure and flattened relic. This problem has bedeviled the understanding of indigenous voices since the coming of the first European record keepers. It affects publications of the most acute anthropologists. It affects the writing and reading of even this present page. The most comprehensive student of America in his time, Jefferson tried to know a vast space, to inhabit with his mind all the continent Seattle sees inhabited by enduring spirits. But to speakers such as Logan or Seattle he can return only what is in effect a very unsatisfying embrace: "Welcome to my library; I would like to accommodate you, on, let me see, yes, that high long shelf over there: Animals, human, North American, rational but uncivilized, oratory of."

Jefferson was a leader of the first generation in an independent America. He was born a British subject, and trained by European masters. His world of learning was the range of printed books and journals in a time that energized bookishness — the age of the *Encyclopédie*, of pamphlet wars leading to the American Revolution, of highly literate constitutional debates in France, England, and America. It was wholly in character for him to mediate between the strange phenomena of this continent and the salons of Paris. It was also his fate to be manifestly out of place himself during much of his life — a provincial contesting an empire, a democratic revolutionary at the French court, an uneasy French-sympathizing statesman in the cabinet of Washington and Hamilton, a slaveholding libertarian, a philosophical scholar in a perfectly regular house in the remote hills of Virginia. To be fair to his particular ways of thinking, we have to make these allowances for his uneasy situation. Holding things in place, and doing that through books and inventories, may well have been his necessary means of survival. The world shifted under his feet through travel, revolution, exploration, shifts of party, and the succession of generations. The spirits most enduring for *him* may well have been his books.

Moreover, it was through books and printed records that Jefferson's own spirit held sway across the continent for many decades. The July 23, 1853, issue of the *Columbian* contains a letter emphatically insisting that new settlers at Alki on "Duwamish Bay" had not been behindhand in celebrating the Fourth of July. They raised a flag, shot off a salute, conducted ceremonies, had a speech, drank some toasts, enjoyed a dinner, and took part in a dance. "The Declaration of Independence was read," the correspondent reports, "and I thought as we stood, hat in hand, listening to the production of the immortal Jefferson, that though few of us, comparatively, were gathered together, we were all duly impressed with the subject and occasion."

But by the 1850s — when Stevens and Seattle met — Jefferson's era had passed. United States territory now extended in a wide band across North America from coast to coast. There had been generations of Americans-since-birth derived from European ancestors. Who, then, was an American "native"? And whose ancestral spirits spoke to and through an articulate dweller on American soil? These questions engaged dozens of American writers in the decades before the Civil War. They inform striking new ways of thinking in the pages of Whitman and Hawthorne.

The opening sections of Whitman's *Leaves of Grass* proclaimed a new voice for America in 1855, a voice that would assimilate all other American voices. "The American poets are to enclose old and new for America is the race of races," Whitman wrote in his preface. "Of them a bard is to be commensurate with a people. To him the other continents arrive as contributions ... he gives them reception for their sake and his own sake. His spirit responds to his country's spirit.... he incarnates its geography and natural life and rivers and lakes."[3] The voice of Whitman's great poem thus purports to draw in other spirits of place, to consolidate all other voices that speak for the landscape. If Jefferson drew in the texts of Indian speech, to place them in his collections of American knowledge, Whitman absorbs them again into a vital refiguring of speech. He writes poetry to be heard and to amplify voices.

Through me many long dumb voices.
Voices of the interminable generations of prisoners and slaves,
Voices of the diseas'd and despairing and of thieves and dwarfs,

---

3. Whitman, 713. The apparent ellipses in these sentences are a peculiarity of Whitman's original punctuation. Quotations from Whitman are cited hereafter by title and line numbers.

Voices of cycles of preparation and accretion,
And of the threads that connect the stars. . . .

Through me forbidden voices,
Voices of sexes and lusts, voices veil'd and I remove the veil,
Voices indecent by me clarified and transfigur'd.

("Song of Myself," 508–12, 516–18)

It is an odd quirk that Whitman creates this new composite voice by being both himself — the rough-clad traveler who had been a Long Island farmer, laborer, and journalist — and a person who exists only on the page, a larger-than-life being constituted of "every atom" in the universe, every part of every reader and of the whole American scene. We can see this new figure emerging in the opening lines of "Song of Myself":

I celebrate myself, and sing myself,
And what I assume you shall assume,
For every atom belonging to me as good belongs to you.

I loafe and invite my soul,
I lean and loafe at my ease observing a spear of summer grass.

But curiously, in later editions of the poem (after 1872) Whitman would present himself in the very next lines with a personal identity much like the one Seattle asserts in his speech — with a pedigree of ancestors long on this land:

My tongue, every atom of my blood, form'd from this soil, this air,
Born here of parents born here from parents the same, and their
    parents the same,

89

I, now thirty-seven years old in perfect health begin,
Hoping to cease not till death.

Creeds and schools in abeyance,
Retiring back a while sufficed at what they are, but never
forgotten,
I harbor for good or bad, I permit to speak at every hazard,
Nature without check with original energy.

The poet seems to thrive on this double nature. Here and now he
loafs and allows nature to speak through him, but at the same
time he retains and even celebrates what he holds "in abeyance" —
the history of a particular and well-schooled self, derived from a
particular (and very literate) tribe.

Later in the poem Whitman's all-inclusiveness extends far beyond such origins. He takes into himself all creeds and schools,
naming religions from around the world. He specifically enfolds
"Manito," a great spirit of American Indians, with Brahma, Buddha, Allah, and Kronos. He literally considers all forms of revelation to be as familiar as the back of his own hand.

Magnifying and applying come I,
Outbidding at the start the old cautious hucksters,
Taking myself the exact dimensions of Jehovah,
Lithographing Kronos, Zeus his son, and Hercules his grandson,
Buying drafts of Osiris, Isis, Belus, Brahma, Buddha,
In my portfolio placing Manito loose, Allah on a leaf, the crucifix
engraved,
With Odin and the hideous-faced Mexitli and every idol and
image,
Taking them all for what they are worth and not a cent more....
Not objecting to special revelations, considering a curl of smoke

or a hair on the back of my hand just as curious as any
revelation....

("Song of Myself," 1026–33, 1039)

These passages do not fully represent the complex range of
Walt Whitman's poetry. But they do address, very directly, the appeal and unique assertions of the Chief Seattle speech. Seattle's
claim to speak for his ancestors, or to have their spirits and hence
their land speak through him; his prophetic paragraphs about the
teachings of competing gods; his assertion that new dwellers on
the land will be surrounded and monitored by his spirits — all
these features find counterpart assertions in *Leaves of Grass*.

Perhaps better said: they meet strong counterassertions in
Whitman's poem. Here is another long inhabitant of America, another heir of American generations, another spokesman for spirits and gods. Only Whitman asserts a voice for the entire continent. In D.H. Lawrence's famous summing up: "The true rhythm
of the American continent [speaks] out in him. He is the first
white aboriginal" (Lawrence, 181–82).

A white aboriginal in America is, of course, an impossibility. At
best Whitman is a self-generating, deeply original poet — if one
can ignore his opening lines about being derived from family, long
habitation, schools, and creeds. Whitman may seem aboriginal,
but his "voice" turns out to be a very cultivated, literary artifice.
The poet's self-conscious literacy shows up clearly in the passage
quoted above, about the way he assumes all gods. He takes them
in as artifacts, or perhaps investments. He "lithographs" some,
"buys drafts" of others, collects Manito and Allah in a portfolio.

In short, assimilation into Whitman's voice is just as distorting
to Indian gods and peoples as is assimilation into Jefferson's library. D.H. Lawrence attacked that side of Whitman very point-

edly: "As soon as Walt *knew* a thing, he assumed a One Identity with it. If he knew that an Eskimo sat in a kyak, immediately there was Walt being little and yellow and greasy, sitting in a kyak." Against this assertion of universal identification Lawrence protests: "I behold no such thing. I behold a rather fat old man full of a rather senile, self-conscious sensuosity" (Lawrence, 174–75).

In fact, Lawrence's rejoinder goes on to point out two failures in Whitman. One is that in his thick volumes of verse and prose there is not much at all about Indians or aboriginals. Edwin Harold Eby's *Concordance* to Whitman's writings lists a few entries, but one turns out to be about a "red girl" Whitman saw in a painting, "The Trapper's Bride" (*Leaves of Grass*, 185–89 and notes). Another is a brief assertion that the poet picks up natural names for the landscape from the breath of departing "red aboriginals": "Leaving such [names] to the States they meet, they depart, charging the land and water with names" ("Starting from Paumanok," 245). Another is a mere mention of "red aborigines" among a list of things the American poet "surrounds" with his spirit ("By Blue Ontario's Shore," 86). For a poet who claims to speak out with the deepest voices of the continent, Whitman is less attentive to Indians than to the freshest immigrants. One looks in vain for direct mention of any Eskimo in a kayak. The closest passage is perhaps a line or two from the opening section of "Fancies at Navesink" about a "pilot in the mist" recalled from a past adventure when "steaming the northern rapids":

Again the trembling, laboring vessel veers me — I press through
    foam-dashed rocks that almost touch me,
Again I mark where aft the small thin Indian helmsman
Looms in the mist, with brow elate and governing hand.

(5–7)

There is a northern body of water here, but a steam vessel instead of a kayak, and an Indian as likely from India as from anywhere in North America.

But Lawrence's larger point is that the ravenous sympathies of Whitman crush out all genuine differences. We may wince at first at Lawrence's version of an Eskimo, but it is a sharp reminder that what feels comfortable to a member of a particular native group will not match the expectations of an outsider reading or writing about the group.

> Walt wasn't an Eskimo. A little, yellow, sly, cunning, greasy little Eskimo. And when Walt blandly assumed Allness, including Eskimoness, unto himself, he was just sucking the wind out of a blown egg-shell, no more. Eskimos are not minor little Walts. They are something that I am not, I know that. Outside the egg of my Allness chuckles the greasy little Eskimo. Outside the egg of Whitman's Allness too.
>
> But Walt wouldn't have it. He was everything and everything was in him. He drove an automobile with a very fierce headlight, along the track of a fixed idea, through the darkness of this world. And he saw everything that way. Just as a motorist does in the night....
>
> ALLNESS! shrieks Walt at a cross-road, going whizz over an unwary Red Indian. (Lawrence, 175–76)

So with Whitman the juggernaut of American literature seems to join the juggernaut of Jefferson's science, to take in and obliterate any voice of an indigenous spirit from the past.

For Nathaniel Hawthorne, writing at about the same time that Whitman began *Leaves of Grass*, voices from the past were not so easy to set aside, hold in abeyance, or blend into a modern self.

Hawthorne was haunted by ancestors, his own ancestors, long on the New England soil, shaping generation after generation to the same patterns of life and livelihood. In *The Scarlet Letter* Hawthorne faces these past generations directly and questions their claims to hold him and his children in bondage forever to a native place. He, too, makes a counterstatement to Seattle's speech, but in a very different tone.

"This old town of Salem — my native place, though I have dwelt much away from it, both in boyhood and maturer years — possesses, or did possess, a hold on my affections, the force of which I never realized during my seasons of actual residence here" (Hawthorne, 40). So Hawthorne writes in the long autobiographical section of his novel, which he titled "The Custom-House."

> And yet, though invariably happiest elsewhere, there is within me a feeling for old Salem, which, in lack of a better phrase, I must be content to call affection. The sentiment is probably assignable to the deep and aged roots which my family has struck into the soil. It is now nearly two centuries and a quarter since the original Briton, the earliest emigrant of my name, made his appearance in the wild and forest-bordered settlement, which has since become a city. And here his descendants have been born and died, and have mingled their earthy substance with the soil; until no small portion of it must necessarily be akin to the mortal frame wherewith, for a little while, I walk the streets. In part, therefore, the attachment which I speak of is the mere sensuous sympathy of dust for dust. Few of my countrymen can know what it is; nor, as frequent transplantation is perhaps better for the stock, need they consider it desirable to know. (40)

Hawthorne goes on to explain that this sentiment has "likewise its moral quality." From boyhood he has felt the presence of his ancestors: "It still haunts me, and induces a sort of home-feeling with the past, which I scarcely claim in reference to the present phase of the town." Hawthorne acknowledges that his Puritan forebears were cruel persecutors as well as upright churchmen. Yet he imagines them judging him as harshly as ever he might judge them, seeing him as a traitor to their earnest and godly seriousness (40–42).

Thus Hawthorne in his way recapitulates the message of Chief Seattle. He speaks for his land, his ancestors, his past generations who have merged with the landscape. He calls up the depths of godly wisdom there. He states that the spirits of the past have endured and will endure there, and will affect the lives of the generations that follow:

> This long connection of a family with one spot, as its place of birth and burial, creates a kindred between the human being and the locality, quite independent of any charm in the scenery or moral circumstances that surround him. It is not love, but instinct. The new inhabitant — who came himself from a foreign land, or whose father or grandfather came — has little claim to be called a Salemite; he has no conception of the oyster-like tenacity with which an old settler, over whom his third century is creeping, clings to the spot where his successive generations have been imbedded. It is no matter that the place is joyless for him; that he is weary of the old wooden houses, the mud and dust, the dead level of site and sentiment, the chill east wind, and the chillest of social atmospheres; — all these, and whatever faults besides he may see or imagine, are nothing to the purpose. The spell survives, and just as powerfully as if the natal spot were an earthly paradise. (42–43)

Nevertheless, Hawthorne deliberately turns away from this pressure of "destiny to make Salem my home." He shakes away the pressure to conform to ancestral patterns. With him, this lineage must cease:

> Nevertheless, this very sentiment is an evidence that the connection, which has become an unhealthy one, should at last be severed. Human nature will not flourish, any more than a potato, if it be planted and replanted, for too long a series of generations, in the same worn-out soil. My children have had other birthplaces, and, so far as their fortunes may be within my control, shall strike their roots into unaccustomed earth. (43)

We must pause to remember that this passage occurs in a haunting novel of New England, with characters drawn from the persecuting ancestral Puritans Hawthorne would like to escape. It is a good question whether Hawthorne ever *could* stand apart from Salem's unhealthy soil. But for present purposes, we must take him at his word. He sees, feels, and embodies an appeal almost identical to Chief Seattle's. And yet, fully conscious of all its worth, he chooses to reject it. Like Whitman he chooses the American ideal of individual autonomy, rather than the sustaining support of family and place. He hedges further when he closes with a wish for his children to "strike their roots" elsewhere. He implies that he, too, would be a forebear, exerting *his* control over subsequent generations and their relations to the land. But in these lines there is still a purposeful urgency to break free of Seattle's appeal: to break free of patterns hallowed by long convention and even wisdom. And of course that urgency also informs the rest of his novel, a tale of a lone heart burning beneath a badge imposed by a united and deeply spiritual people.

Notes on the State of Virginia is a classic of American science, politics, and geography. *Leaves of Grass* and *The Scarlet Letter* are classics of American literature. They are embedded in what many other writers and thinkers have had to know about the continent and the possibilities of life here. What we commonly call American politics, learning, and literature are inconceivable without these books. And the passages we have just surveyed are not incidental but central to their main themes and strategies. Taken together they push back against Seattle's speech with massive force. They work to anticipate its appeal, categorize it, assimilate it, or directly reject it. They may show how deeply obtuse the highly literate can be in supposing that they have heard or understood voices of the spirit of this land. Or we may regard them as merely works that speak from afar; they just happen to address their returns very neatly to the voice of a Far Western Indian. But together they do not miss the point of Seattle's message. Their language and their pressure are incorporated in what readers have long had to heed as voices from the American past. They overwhelm Seattle's speech in what many think of as American history and culture.

Moreover, these passages bear directly on the ways Isaac Stevens dealt with Indians in the West. They not only anticipate general attitudes of an official American representative, but also prefigure and closely parallel Stevens's personal idiosyncracies. They help explain his simultaneous sympathies and indifferences to Indian speeches and Indian claims. But that subject calls for treatment by itself.

CHAPTER 5

The Answers of Governor Stevens

ISAAC STEVENS is a thorny character in the history of Washington Territory. To some he was a hero — a dynamic, decisive leader who outlined far-seeing policies and followed through with sensible force and persistence. But to many he was a bustling, ambitious, hard-driving, arrogant authoritarian — a martinet to subordinates, an assertive rival to other high officials, an empire builder ruthlessly overturning the lives and holdings of Indians who stood in his way. Even his sympathetic modern biographer allows that "his temperament, training, and professional career best prepared him to operate as a monarch" (Richards, 275). By the spring of 1856, some of his closest associates were complaining about him in the same terms. He had been governor for barely three years, but they saw him as "actuated by an arrogant and unbridled love of power that unfits him for any trust in which life or liberty is concerned." In these words they wrote to the secretary of state, petitioning that Stevens be dismissed as governor. The same charges spread in print, when such letters were copied in the *New York Times* and other newspapers.[1]

This crisis in his career grew directly out of his treaty-making policies. After completing his tour of treaty councils around Puget Sound, he had moved east, to further councils beyond the Cascade Mountains, and even beyond the Continental Divide. But in the fall of 1855, while he was still negotiating, war broke out

---

1. George Gibbs and Hugh Goldsborough to William H. Marcy, May 11, 1856, quoted in Richards, 281–82; *New York Times* (August 7, 1856), 8.

between Indians and settlers in areas he had tried to control. Prospectors invading Yakima lands were murdered; so was the agent Stevens had appointed for the tribes between the Cascades and the Bitterroots. Soon violence had spread across the territory, and it persisted through the winter that followed. Settlers at Puget Sound lived in terror under the shadow of blockhouses and other hastily arranged defenses.

In facing this emergency Stevens clearly overreached his authority. He made his way back to Olympia, called up a force of local militia, and ordered the evacuation of all Indians from the eastern side of the Sound. He asserted emergency powers as both governor and superintendent of Indian affairs — and soon landed in awkward conflicts with other American authorities. He demanded support from the regular army. But General John E. Wool, the commander of the department of the Pacific, replied from San Francisco that he could not send forces sufficient to do all that Stevens had in mind. In fact he rebuked the governor on several grounds — for taking unwarranted command of military forces, for encouraging settlement of lands better left to the Indians, and for perpetuating Indian wars for political and economic gain. Wool, too, prosecuted his attacks not only in private and official correspondence but also in public media; he arranged the publication of a full-page manifesto back in Washington, D.C., in the pages of the *National Intelligencer* (Melina, 123–36).

Meanwhile, Stevens confronted civilians closer to home. He suspected that half-breeds living at Muck Prairie near Olympia were giving supplies and shelter to marauding Indians. He ordered their arrest and later their trial by a military tribunal. When civilian courts issued writs of habeas corpus, he pushed matters to extremes by declaring martial law, sending troops into the courtroom, even arresting and imprisoning a territorial judge. In the end, Stevens had to back down from these high-handed and dramatic confrontations. But by May 1856 he had thoroughly embroiled himself in national controversies. His behavior was at the center of debates about the powers and excesses of territorial governors.

He thus made many enemies and stirred up lasting resentments. Acrimony poisons many accounts of his time in the territory. He sought endorsement of a kind by running for office in 1857 and winning election as the territorial delegate to Congress. A majority of voters seemed to agree that he was not an utterly deplorable public official. But by then he had also turned friends into active adversaries, who would keep on charging that he had been drunk, deranged, and incompetent in his official conduct. Fifty years later, that resentment still smoldered in the recollections of many pioneers. Ezra Meeker, for example, wrote a substantial book accusing Stevens of judicial murder for the hanging of Leschi, one of the leaders of Indian attacks in western Washington. Meeker ascribed much of Stevens's outrageous conduct to chronic alcoholism. He cited his own personal recollections, and he quoted contemporary letters to the press: "That in his fits of intoxication he knew no bounds to his language and his actions, almost everyone who has had official connection with him is aware."[2]

Richards points out that charges of drunkenness were commonplace slanders in political contests of the nineteenth century, and that no such charges were made against Stevens before the Indian Wars and Stevens's confrontation with the judges in 1856 (Richards, 289). But from then on, Stevens and his bottle were

---

2. George Gibbs, letter to the *Washington Republican* (June 5, 1857), quoted in Meeker, 55.

read backwards into the record. He appeared intoxicated "on important public occasions," George Gibbs wrote in 1857 and Ezra Meeker repeated in 1905: "at Fort Colville, at the treaties here on the Sound, at the Blackfeet Council, and more lately at that with the Nez Perces" (Meeker, 54–55).

Whether intoxicated or not, Stevens stands indicted in history as a hasty, reckless leader, who came to Puget Sound and suddenly forced inadequate treaties upon settlers and Indians who until then had been living in comparative harmony (Trafzer, 4, 19–36). He sowed injustice, violence, death, and devastation. In short, his implied answer to the pleas of Chief Seattle was an insensitive assertion of force — force of law, if that would serve, force of arms, if not.

But Stevens demands to be understood in wider contexts than just his term as territorial governor. In fact, he presents a particularly interesting character because it is hard to fit or confine him in just one tidy role anywhere in his ambitious career.

One brief passage in Seattle's speech brings this complexity into relief: "There is little in common between us. The ashes of our ancestors are sacred and their final resting place is hallowed ground, while you wander away from the tombs of your fathers seemingly without regret." Addressed as they are to Stevens, as the official representing thousands of invaders, these lines raise searching questions. What motives brought this particular man thousands of miles from the place of his birth? What homeland did he imagine he was loyal to, and in what ways?

Seattle's speech goes on to spell out his people's ways of relating to a sacred earth. Every landmark, literally every hillside, valley, plain, and grove "has been hallowed by some fond memory or some sad experience of my tribe." Not only experiences of the living but also the ashes of the dead enrich the Puget Sound region. "The very dust under your feet responds more lovingly to our footsteps than to yours, because it is the ashes of our ancestors, and our bare feet are conscious of the sympathetic touch, for the soil is rich with the life of our kindred." What is more, the spirits of the dead remain immanent there and will remain forever. Seattle thus seems to inhabit two interrelated worlds at the same time: the here-and-now world of forests and valleys, and an eternal spirit world that affectionately embraces these mundane features.

By contrast, Stevens's actions seem to imply a shallower conception of the universe — a more cynical outlook on here-and-now reality, which was to be managed by political and military means. But in fact Stevens, too, lived in a world of overlapping realities. As an ambitious, intellectual, nineteenth-century American he had learned to inhabit many different settings. Most to the point, his years in Washington Territory were a constant exercise in balancing his loyalties, in living in many dimensions at the same time. Both officially and privately he tested many simultaneous human identities in the physical geography of North America.

The attitudes we have seen in the preceding chapter, in the passages and situations of Jefferson, Whitman, and Hawthorne, merge in the figure of Isaac Stevens. He understood his main work as furthering what Jefferson had set in motion — the integration of the Far West into the political and intellectual frameworks of the eastern United States. At the same time, he developed an ego that could fairly rival Whitman's. He had a driving ambition to assimilate an entire continent into his own personal experience and power, and thereby find a very high place for himself in the recognition of his people. Finally, like Hawthorne, he contemplated a personal move far from New England as a restorative development for his family. He thereby initiated commitments at Puget Sound and elsewhere, so that his people would trace *his* deeds and footsteps as ancestral precedents.

Like Jefferson, Stevens was an intellectual polymath as well as a politician. He came to Washington Territory intent on seeing into the West as well as responding forcefully to the problems of government it presented. We have already seen that Stevens was an assiduous reader and writer, a builder of libraries, and a disciplined keeper of records. He was first in his class at West Point (1839) because he forced himself to learn subjects that did not come easily, such as French and drawing; he became a wide reader later because he felt the defects of his training as an engineer. But he was also gifted with a wide outlook combined with a keen eye for detail. Before he came west he had seen action with the Corps of Engineers in Mexico, then in Washington, D.C., administered the Coastal Survey, the agency that compiled accurate new geographical information to produce maps, charts, and navigational tables. He was thus trained and experienced in the strategic geography of all of North America. At the national capital he had pushed his way into sufficient notice that, at the age of thirty-five, he held three simultaneous appointments under the new administration of Franklin Pierce: governor of the newly created Washington Territory, responsible to the secretary of state; superintendent of Indian affairs for the territory, responsible to the secretary of the interior; and chief of the survey for a northern railway route, preparing his reports for the secretary of war.

As he came west with an exploring party along the course of the Upper Missouri, Stevens knew that he was retracing the route of Lewis and Clark. At one point, in the Bitterroot Valley of what is now western Montana, Stevens recorded this debt with pleasure:

"Fort Owen is situated on the Scattering Creek of Lewis and Clark. It was a matter of the greatest gratification, with their narrative in hand, to pass through this valley and realize the fidelity and graphic character of their descriptions."[3] Part of Stevens's gratification may have been knowing that he was enlarging the project Lewis and Clark had begun. But whereas they had been army officers under full and exacting directions from President Jefferson, Stevens was very much his own commander. He, too, exercised military discipline, even as a civilian official. And as he had gone about securing his appointments, he had urged, specified, and even written out terms and objectives of his own (Hazard Stevens, *Life*, 1:292).

Stevens aimed to understand the Far West in a comprehensive view, to amass, refine, and publish a wealth of new information. He staffed his expedition with other military officers who were trained engineers. He also brought artists, naturalists, a meteorologist, and a geologist. His modern biographer explains that there were four different exploration parties examining possible railroad routes to the West.

> But Stevens more than any other survey leader assumed the task of providing complete geographic, geologic, botanic, zoologic, and meteorologic information for an area of several hundred thousand square miles. . . . Stevens was determined that the northern railroad survey would be the greatest scientific, topographic expedition since Lewis and Clark and would provide a fitting opening chapter to the new era about to dawn in the northwest quarter of the nation. (Richards, 102)

---

3. Hazard Stevens, *Life*, 1:380. Stevens was using the narrative of Lewis and Clark first published in 1814 and reading entries for September 8 and 9, 1805. See Coues, 2:588.

In practical terms, he had to coordinate several teams of explorers and personally experience all the hardships of a trek from St. Paul to Fort Vancouver. Rough travel, short rations, grumbling subordinates, broken instruments, defective equipment, heat, cold, mosquitoes, anxieties about Indians and wild animals — Stevens faced them all, just as Lewis and Clark did. Though his feet were shod, as Seattle's speech claims, Stevens in fact felt the contours of the West with special sensitivity. One of his feet had been badly torn up by a bullet in the Mexican War, so that he walked with a special boot. He also suffered from an abdominal hernia, which had put him out of action for weeks in Mexico and doubled him up when he tried to ride a horse.

Nevertheless he pushed on across the country. When he ran out of funds, he kept this project going anyhow by authorizing further explorations and taking artists and scientists with him on his treaty-making travels. Jefferson had his *Notes on the State of Virginia*; Lewis and Clark had their published history of exploration; by 1859, Stevens had turned out his comprehensive, final two-volume railroad *Reports* — a monument of detailed learning about the Northwest, from Minnesota to the Pacific.

William Goetzmann notes that its results were unfortunately buried in an official congressional document few scientists would consult, and that it lacked the penetration of a single synthetic genius: "The whole report represented a cooperative enterprise that made generalization difficult. There was no Darwin to ruminate over all the data and make the grand generalization. The result was order on a lower level. No attempt had been made to apply the findings to the solution of an ultimate problem. Instead the data was classified, grouped, filed, and pigeonholed for future reference" (Goetzmann, 336–37). Stevens's main argument also failed; a northern railway route was in the end rejected by the secretary of war, and its advantages were disputed by many of Stevens's own subordinates (282-83).

But his reports still have their merits. According to a modern expert, Stevens was a very respectable geographer. He saw possibilities in new regions that others overlooked or wrote off, blinded by preconceptions or the dismissive remarks of earlier explorers (Meinig, "Isaac Stevens," 542–52). He also fostered extensive records about Indians of the Pacific Northwest. George Gibbs, who furnished much of this material, labored to collect vocabularies of many Indian languages as well as the Chinook Jargon; he later published his researches as a principal ethnologist at the Smithsonian Institution.[4] Gibbs also gathered reports of Indian legends and composed one of the earliest accounts of Northwest Indian mythology — though that account lay in manuscript until 1955 (Ella E. Clark, "George Gibbs' Account"). Finally, Stevens pressed to make a visual record of the region he was mapping. He appointed John Mix Stanley as the artist for his railway survey. Later he discovered the talents of Private Gustav Sohon, who excelled Stanley as an artist and made the only known likenesses of many Indians.[5] A modern historian concludes a survey of the expedition's art with high praise for its leader's foresight:

> Given the fact that the Lewis and Clark expedition, unlike its contemporaneous counterparts in maritime exploration, did not systematically produce drawings of the landscapes encountered in the trek across the continent, we owe the first substantive views of the northwestern frontier to the man who followed in their foot-

---

4. Gibbs's career has been surveyed in Beckham, "George Gibbs."

5. Sohon's works, now preserved at the Washington State Historical Society, have been reproduced in Nicandri, *Northwest Chiefs*. A selection is also included in Hazard Stevens, *Life*.

steps fifty years later. With the possible exception of Paul Kane, no more significant body of imagery was produced in the greater Northwest before the era of sophisticated photography than that which flows from the direct or adjunct influences of Isaac Stevens. (Nicandri, "Isaac I. Stevens," 148)

Of course, exploring and studying the land, mapping it, and describing it, were not at all the same as enlarging a political empire or establishing and defending a settlement. But as Stevens took up his other offices, he could have felt Jefferson's influence weighing over him in these matters, too. Was the United States to acquire and hold territory in the Far West, and to compete with other empires in trade across the Pacific? Jefferson had foreseen and initiated exactly these lines of policy. Were new territories to be settled and developed, for eventual establishment as new states? Jefferson had helped establish that design in a 1784 plan reported to Congress, which led to the Northwest Ordinance of 1787. It was under the terms of these arrangements that Stevens became the federally appointed governor. Were Indians to be allotted restricted lands and kept apart from white settlements; or were they to be encouraged to adapt to settled agriculture, trades, and manufactures in preparation for eventual assimilation? When Stevens proposed treaties incorporating these two contrary lines of policy, he echoed official positions Jefferson had proclaimed decades earlier.[6]

In other words, Stevens, too, had to acknowledge ancestral spirits abroad in the land. Their words, deeds, and legacies were the forces that had brought him to treaty councils. Not Jefferson

---

6. A good, brief discussion of Jefferson's policies can be found at the opening of a cogent chapter, "Shoving the Indians Out of the Way," in Meinig, *Continental America*, 78–103.

alone, but scores of deceased American predecessors had developed the Constitution, treaties, and a complex body of laws and precedents for western development. It was with their authority and within their restrictions that Stevens did what he did.

If he tried to evade or overstep those limits, he risked immediate retribution. As we have seen, General Wool in San Francisco, or judges and political rivals close at hand, could do more than object and create immediate frustrations. Through the press they could also make loud reverberations from coast to coast.

To make matters worse, Stevens had to conflate his scientific and political views — and thus discover that the new laws that had brought him west did not neatly correspond to the realities of geography. Congress might confirm treaties and carve out a new Washington Territory between the Columbia River and the forty-ninth parallel, but it could not thereby eradicate settled ways that had developed for a century and more. The Hudson's Bay Company had withdrawn its main posts to Vancouver Island, but within Washington Territory it still claimed some landholdings and trading rights by treaty, some of its former employees chose to stay (and claimed their own holdings), and there remained disputed territories such as the San Juan Islands. Catholic missionaries remained at little enclaves around the territory, another legacy of old fur-trading empires across what is now Canada. At Puget Sound, the Indians consisted of many groups in many locations, speaking many different languages. They lived by seasonal fishing and gathering. They could not be readily segregated and resettled on one or two large reservations. But new bands of settlers were already arriving in numbers. Wagon trains of them were on the Oregon Trail, heading for the Willamette Valley in Oregon, and arriving to find better prospects a little to the north. The California gold rush of 1849 had carried thousands to the West Coast. Gold rushes to Colville in eastern Washington in 1855 and to British Columbia in 1858 were to bring more rowdy adventurers. Settlements such as Seattle and Olympia were already being marked on the map and built up with houses, streets, mills, and stores. How were new settlers to stake their claims and hold clear title to their lands?

Clearly, Stevens was sent west to face this problem. At his back was the will of Congress, to open a major railroad line to the Pacific. And even more forcefully, there were new laws on the books, to establish clear land titles within a very limited period of time.

The Oregon Donation Land Act of 1850 enabled a male settler to claim 160 acres for himself and another 160 for his wife. (Settlers already in Oregon before 1850 could claim up to 640 acres.) Similar laws continued to govern settlement in Washington Territory after it became separated from Oregon in 1852. The Donation Acts were specifically designed to "induce settlements on the public domain in distant or dangerous portions of the nation." But they also had a time limit — claims had to be filed by December 1, 1855. No one explained how lands could be claimed at all before Indian title was removed (Donaldson, 295–96). Settlers simply came and made their clearings. When Indians began to respond with raids and uprisings, the newcomers resorted to lynch law.

Stevens grasped this situation as soon as he reached Olympia. He wrote back to the office of Indian Affairs in late 1853, pressing the urgent necessity for making treaties with the Indians west of the Cascades:

> For years they have been promised payment for their lands by the whites; and they have waited with an abiding faith that the whites would redeem their many promises. For the last two years, however, the great numbers of settlers, who have located in this Terri-

tory, has made them suspicious and uneasy; and they upbraid the whites for want of faith. The lands of all the Indians from the Columbia river to the 49° of latitude, west of the Cascade mountains, are so fast becoming settled by the whites, that, within another year, there will hardly be a choice claim of land on the sound, or the different streams, but what will be located upon by settlers; and thus the Indians will be driven from their homes. Even within the last year the population of the Territory has increased from two to five thousand; and that without the aid of a road across the Cascade mountains, until late in the season, and which was almost entirely cut out by the unaided exertion of the citizens. (Isaac I. Stevens to George W. Manypenny, 6)

Stevens probably exaggerated some numbers here. He wrote to seek a large appropriation for treaty-making, and as governor he also pursued money for road building if not railroad building. But his letter goes on to note the precise legal dilemmas facing new settlers. The intercourse law of 1834 prohibited white invasion of Indian territories. Yet the Donation Act specifically opened these lands for settlement claims. For Stevens, the only solution lay in immediately and directly negotiating treaties with the forty tribes of the Puget Sound basin, "extinguishing their titles, and placing them on reservations where they can be cared for and attended to." His letter notes that the Indians were willing to sell their lands but unwilling to move out of Puget Sound. He reports discussions with the oldest, most experienced settlers, but also sees the need for a closer survey of the land and all its resources, to prevent future strife. He argues that such explorations should be funded and begin at once (ibid., 6–9).

In this light, it would seem that Stevens acted prudently and responsibly in his haste to conclude treaties. In his boots who could have done differently in good conscience? Before him were

Indians seeking settlement for lands already snatched from them. Behind him was the pressure of law, politics, westward migration, and even a projected railroad. And time was running out. Not only would Donation Claims have to be filed within a few years; Stevens himself had a limited term of office, as did the federal officials who had sent him west and who would have to confirm and ratify his treaties. This situation seemed to demand someone gifted at attacking problems incisively and with constant energy — in short a man exactly like Stevens, used to the exercise of military authority in undertaking large projects and forcing them to efficient completion.

There may be grounds for reproaching Stevens, even so, for extreme haste and questionable methods in his treaty making: arriving suddenly, sending out surveyors, assembling councils, dictating terms in a language that had to be translated on the spot, waiting to hear Indians' minor objections and modifications, but somehow getting marks on paper within a few hours or days at most, and then moving on to make another survey with other tribes. But again we should ask, what alternatives were available in Washington Territory in 1854? Stevens was constrained not only by time and the pressures of Manifest Destiny; he was also limited in his resources as governor and in the kind of backing he could reasonably expect from the federal government.

As the Indian Wars demonstrated, Stevens could command only limited manpower even in an emergency. He had no large staff to study Indians and their ways and work out more enlightened policies or treaties. Instead he had to rely on a few local advisors and subordinates. Few of these were deeply acquainted with Indian customs or needs. The agents Stevens appointed often turned out to be incompetent or untrustworthy. Even the best talents at hand could be callous in their attitudes.

A good case in point is George Gibbs, a principal figure in the Puget Sound treaty councils. He was the official surveyor who scouted and marked off reservation lands, and he acted as council secretary, writing up the official records of the treaty meetings. Gibbs was also the author of a formal report on Indians of the region, which Stevens would publish in his Pacific railroad *Reports* and recopy in his own report to the commissioner of Indian affairs.[7] It is hard to know how closely Stevens could have trusted him, for Gibbs was a disappointed Whig officeholder — in other words, a potential adversary in local politics, for Stevens remained a sturdy Democrat. In fact, as we have already seen, Gibbs did turn against Stevens after the Indian Wars, and even called for his removal from office. Gibbs is just as hard to read in his direct dealings with Indians. On the one hand, he was fascinated by their languages and customs. He went out of his way to record accounts of mythology and ceremonial practices. On the other hand, he wrote a report for Stevens in 1854 advocating court martial procedures and exemplary punishments for Indians, such as execution on the spot for murder, whipping and shaving of the

---

7. George Gibbs to George B. McClellan, March 4, 1854, in Isaac I. Stevens, *Reports*, 427–34; Isaac I. Stevens to George W. Manypenny, Sept. 16, 1854, in Manypenny, 447–57. One of the most notorious remarks of Stevens about Indians is thus directly attributable to Gibbs. It refers to Chinook and Cowlitz Indians who were already ravaged by disease and alcoholism: "The speedy extinction of the race seems rather to be hoped for than regretted, and they look forward to it themselves with a sort of indifference" (Gibbs, in Stevens, *Reports*, 429; Stevens, in Manypenny, 449). In both texts there immediately follows a notable further statement: "The duty of the government, however, is not affected by their vices, for these they owe in great measure to our own citizens. If it can do nothing else, it can at least aid in supporting them while they survive."

head for robbery: "In case of any resistance or refusal the chastise-
ment may however be signal. A single severe lesson of this kind
will probably be effectual in quelling not merely these, but the
tribes of the whole sound, & prevent a recurrence of such affairs."
In case the governor missed the point, Gibbs sent him a letter
later in the year, suggesting that when an Indian criminal could
not be found or convicted in court, the chief or his tribe should be
compelled to furnish a substitute for punishment.[8]

Stevens had to work in apparent harmony with men such as
this if he was to accomplish anything at all. He also had to gauge
what the United States government would agree to support. As he
knew from long experience, federal resources were limited and often released from a stingy hand. What he, Gibbs, and a small
treaty commission worked out was a model treaty based on recent treaties with the Ottoe, Missouri, and Omaha Indians.[9]

But could any sort of treaty be devised to the lasting advantage
of Indians? That was a nice legal question even in Stevens's day.
Did not western lands belong to the United States already, by purchase and conquest? Were not treaties, at best, supplementary arrangements, offering merely prudent, humanitarian concessions?
The Supreme Court had decided cases along these lines, and held
further that American Indians were not foreign nations but (in
Chief Justice John Marshall's memorable words) "domestic dependent nations": "They occupy a territory to which we assert a title
independent of their will, which must take effect in point of pos-

---

8. Gibbs to Stevens, February 7 and October 2, 1854, National Archives
Microfilm Publication M5, roll 23, frames 0043 and 0112.

9. Records of the Proceedings of the Commission to hold Treaties with
the Indian Tribes of Washington Territory and the Blackfoot Country,
National Archives Microfilm Publication T494, reel 5, frame 0171.

session when their right of possession ceases. Meanwhile they are in a state of pupillage. Their relation to the United States resembles that of a ward to his guardian" (Cherokee Nation v. Georgia, 5 Peters 15–20, in Prucha, 59). The effect of these words was that Indians could not bring suit to enforce their treaties or prohibit encroachments on them by state governments. In 1856 the federal commissioner of Indian affairs, George Manypenny, reported to Congress that since 1853 the United States had negotiated fifty-two separate Indian treaties and acquired 174 million acres of land. "In no equal period of our history have so many treaties been made, or such vast accessions of land been established."[10] In the next paragraph, the commissioner lamented that "the existing laws for the protection of the persons and property of the Indian wards of the government are sadly defective." He could do little more than hope that the Congress might act to alleviate this problem. There are three plain implications of his report: that treaties were negotiated mainly for acquiring land, that Stevens was one of many negotiating agents in a new burst of western settlement in the 1850s, and that Indians as "wards of the government" could hope for little in these transactions.

Of course it was in Stevens's interest to make treaties that would hold, securing peaceful settlement and some hope of Indian safety and prosperity. It cannot be denied that he did achieve this aim, at least in part. Later, in the twentieth century, the Puget Sound treaties resulted in landmark court decisions — and in public outcry about what Stevens did *for* the Indians. Rulings of the United States District Court in 1974, later confirmed by the

---

10. *Annual Report of the Commissioner of Indian Affairs*, Senate Executive Document no. 5, 34th Congress, 3rd session, serial 875, pp. 571–75, quoted in Prucha, 90.

Supreme Court, reaffirmed treaty provisions giving Indians inviolable fishing rights, including a 50 percent share of the annual salmon run.[11] In these cases, as in many others, tribes that could claim treaty recognition have fared far better than others.

But even with all these qualifications and extenuations, Stevens seems an unhappy late embodiment of Jeffersonian policies and practices. A half century after Jefferson he was brought face to face with what that president had been able to hold at a comfortable distance. Like Jefferson, Stevens asserted and defended American claims to the Northwest and worked to draw that region into the domain of literate civilization, scientific learning, and established federal laws. But unlike Jefferson, Stevens had to do that by directly meeting, cajoling, and even coercing the illiterate. He secured the needed marks on paper. He got his treaties and once more put Indians at a safe distance by recording their capitulations in black and white. He got his heavy volumes of railroad *Reports*, as well. But both kinds of literate achievement could turn out to be paper thin. They did not prevent a war, after all, or build a railroad. And after a very few years they began gathering dust in government archives.

---

11. United States v. State of Washington (384 *Federal Supplement* 312). A full general treatment of the background and consequences of the Boldt decision, see Cohen, *Treaties on Trial*. The decision continues to excite controversy from year to year as its provisions affect particular tribes, regions, and fishing practices. It should be noted that the origins of this decision were not simple and placid legal maneuvers but "a continuing and escalating series of fishing rights controversies" in the fall of 1970. Violent confrontations between Indians and armed police created national publicity. As a result of this pressure, Vine Deloria writes, the federal government intervened and pressed the cases that resulted in the Boldt ruling (Deloria, 12).

The question remains: Why did Stevens choose to become an agent of empire in the Far West? To repeat the words of Seattle's speech, why did he personally decide to "wander away from the tombs of [his] fathers seemingly without regret" and invade the lands that Indians held sacred? Some simple answers suggest themselves immediately: fortune, fame, political power, or even the excitement of adventure. But another depth of Stevens emerges if we consider him as a contemporary of Walt Whitman, and as an ambitious political counterpart to Whitman the ambitious American poet. We have seen Walt Whitman asserting a powerful self to assimilate all the peoples and voices of America, to refine them into a song of his own and thus give back a common poem to his contemporaries. In a parallel effort of self-assertion, Stevens was working to assimilate everything that could be known about the vast new northwestern region of the country, with an eye to building a political base there for long service at the highest levels of government. Like Whitman, and like many energetic young men of his time, he was exercising a new sense of identity. Call it patriotic egotism. He was measuring both a self and a newly enlarged nation at the same time, thrusting his boots into stirrups and scratching his pen across paper to gain power and recognition across the continent.

His biographer, Kent Richards, points out that Stevens understood this line of ambition at the time of his appointment. "If Stevens could gain command of the railroad survey as well as the governorship of the new territory, development of the Northwest and the expansion of his own power and influence would be virtually limitless. He might become the spokesman for the Pacific Northwest as William Henry Harrison and Thomas Hart Benton had been representative of earlier frontiers" (Richards, 96). If his deeds could gain sufficient respect, way might open to a congressional or senate seat or a cabinet office or other national prominence for years to come.

This idea derived not only from regional figures in earlier national politics, such as Harrison, Benton, Henry Clay, Daniel Webster, and John C. Calhoun. Stevens had long measured himself against ambitious contemporaries, too. It was an urgent pressure of his training and early career. At West Point he competed for highest standing in his class. As a young officer, he yearned for duties and signal accomplishments that would prove his mettle and boost his rank. In the Mexican campaigns he gladly displayed his prowess as a newly trained engineer. Afterwards, he led a lobbying campaign in Washington, to secure full pay and seniority for engineering officers who had received brevet promotions. From his first days in uniform, Stevens was groomed to serve and rise as a well-trained officer of the United States. When he reached Washington to serve in the Coastal Survey, he could readily see that he was as intelligent and informed as many others in high office. He also began to make connections to put himself there.

At every stage of his early career, he can be found among leaders of his generation. At West Point his closest rival was Henry Halleck, who not only served later as Lincoln's general-in-chief, but also achieved distinction before the Civil War as a lawyer in California and an authority in military theory and international law. In Mexico, Stevens was one of a small corps of army engineers, which included Robert E. Lee, P. G. T. Beauregard, and George B. McClellan; Stevens later appointed McClellan to conduct the survey of western Washington for his railroad *Reports*. In Washington he made friends with politicians interested in western territories, such as his fellow Democrat, Stephen A. Douglas. For a time he boarded in a rooming house with Commodore Matthew Perry. While Stevens was making his way to the West Coast to help establish Washington Territory, Perry was on his way to make treaties, by force if necessary, in Japan.

Active promotion of American ideals across the continent and around the world took on the label "Young America" in this period. In 1852 this name described a movement of younger Democrats to nominate Douglas for president; their issues remained vital in the campaign of Franklin Pierce, who actually ran and won. "The grand ideas which are most potent in the election," a supporter wrote to Pierce that summer, "are sympathy for the liberals of Europe, the expansion of the American republic southward and westward, and the grasping of the magnificent purse of the commerce of the Pacific, in short the ideas for which the term *Young America* is the symbol" (Edmund Burke to Franklin A. Pierce, June 14, 1852, in Curti, 45). Stevens campaigned for Pierce and clearly profited from his victory. Railroad surveys, territorial settlements, a new drive to make Indian treaties, Perry's mission across the Pacific — all were initiatives that promptly fulfilled Young America aspirations.

Young America was also a larger term, a commonplace idea of the preceding decade. Merle Curti has traced its coinage to a commencement address of 1845 (Curti, 34). But many of the same geographical and political notions can be found in Ralph Waldo Emerson's 1844 address "The Young American" and many other writings of the period. Emerson celebrated the development of railroads for the promise it opened of rapidly assimilating all older creeds into an improved "American sentiment": "Not only is distance annihilated, but when, as now, the locomotive and the steamboat, like enormous shuttles, shoot every day across the thousand various threads of national descent and employment, and bind them fast in one web, an hourly assimilation goes forward, and there is no danger that local peculiarities and hostilities should be preserved." With the new power of commerce, he went on, immigrants to the New World were crowding westward "to the prairie and the mountains" and contributing to make American law and institutions "more catholic and cosmopolitan" than those of any other country:

> It seems so easy for America to inspire and express the most expansive and humane spirit; new-born, free, healthful, strong, the land of the laborer, of the democrat, of the philanthropist, of the believer, of the saint, she should speak for the human race. It is the country of the Future. From Washington, proverbially "the city of magnificent distances," through all its cities, states and territories, it is a country of beginnings, of projects, of designs, and expectations.[12]

These ideas of Manifest Destiny (a term coined at about the same time) were joined with an emphasis on youth. "I call upon you, young men, to obey your heart and be the nobility of this land," Emerson exhorted. "Who should lead the leaders, but the Young American?" (Emerson, 226). Policies of commercial expansion, territorial development, modern technology, and liberal agitation against conservative regimes are combined again and again, in editorials and political speeches of this period, with the celebration of young men in a young nation. In the preceding chapter we saw the assimilationist pressure of Whitman's poetry; Whitman's newspaper editorials of the late 1840s were frequently Young American (Brasher, 85–95, 103–4, 238).

For Stevens, then, the schooled ambition of his early career converged with a widespread American sentiment in the early

---

12. "The Young American: A Lecture read before the Mercantile Library Association, Boston, February 7, 1844," in Emerson, 213, 217.

1850s. Both national expansion and personal drives for power were being fostered as patriotic virtues. Not everyone had supported the war in Mexico or limitless annexation of new territories, but a national election campaign had just rung with self-justifying idealism. Victory opened new opportunities. And leading intellectuals as well as political propagandists were extolling the idea of young men winning the West.

For our purposes, these developments point to a very particular question: What were the personal costs of such ambitions? National expansion proved devastating for Indians; what were its strains on a man such as Stevens himself? To prove himself to his people, a leader like Seattle could call on old loyalties to his family, shared experiences in war and danger, and familiar, direct acquaintance through the years. Not so, for a Young American. To "lead the leaders" as Emerson suggested, meant constant, risky rivalry with scores or hundreds of other young talents and egos, to win high rank and influence over millions of people.

Stevens is an especially revealing figure in this regard, because he had only his own talents to rely on and his appointments were not spectacularly promising. He had no developed political support in a particular home state or district. His army career had stalled in peacetime, after the end of the Mexican War. Unlike Robert E. Lee, he could not claim lineage from an old and distinguished family. Nor could he claim alliance with a powerful patron — as, for example, John C. Frémont could, after eloping with the daughter of Senator Benton. Stevens had to seize and make the most of opportunity when it knocked. And in 1853 a territorial governorship was not regarded as an especially portentous plum. Richards explains that such posts "went, as a general rule, to mediocrities" (97). To make it into his main chance, Stevens had to secure concurrent appointments — as the leader of a railroad survey and a superintendent of Indian affairs — and define his own terms for conspicuous accomplishment.

As the next few years proved, Stevens put himself far, far out on a political limb. Emerson might speak glowingly of railroads and steamboats annihilating space and time and weaving America into a solid fabric like shuttles in a power loom. Washington Territory proved otherwise. To get there overland, Stevens had to organize a special expedition from St. Paul, with each man responsible for breaking in his own mule! To get back and forth by the most advanced means still took many weeks — by steamer between the Columbia River and San Francisco, to connect with other ships to Panama, and from there to either New Orleans or a port on the East Coast. Sailing connections were chancy, and the Panama crossing was a torment. The trip was too hazardous for Stevens's wife and children to make without him. When they did come west, in 1854, two daughters went astray for a time in the Panama jungle and four members of the family came down with yellow fever.

Communication between east and west faced the same hazards and hardships. If getting to Olympia required daring and physical endurance, building a political career there also demanded ingenuity, cunning, and a full measure of good luck. Orders and instructions from the administration might be changed or countermanded before they arrived in the West. Reports or replies might be out of date by the time they got back to Washington. Or they might simply go astray and vanish. Stevens had to travel himself to be effective in the federal capital. And while he spent weeks or months on one coast, he risked losing whatever authority, control, and progress he had labored to build up on the other. This is an old story in American politics. It continues to bedevil congressmen from the West even in a time of jet travel and instant communications. But for Stevens everything depended on lengthy and precise exchanges of words. He could survey a railroad route in months, but it took years to get a report into print — let alone to get one spike driven. He could push ahead with treaty councils, but full ratification depended on slow-moving bureaus and committees far away. A Young American could grow old waiting for his good works to gain due recognition.

And even if they succeeded, what then? Stevens did make tangible accomplishments within a few years. His treaties were ratified. His reports were published. His controversial term as governor resulted in at least local reaffirmation and election to two terms as territorial delegate in Congress. But by the end of the second term it was 1860, and national politics had changed, changed utterly.

As a Democrat, Stevens had continued to make himself a conspicuous writer and organizer. But in 1860 he reached ambitiously once more, and courted disaster. He let territorial concerns take second place for a few months, to put his efforts into presidential politics. By midsummer he was chairman of the Democratic National Party Executive Committee — in other words, a chief organizer for the Breckinridge-Lane campaign. But after the election of Lincoln, he was nobody. Back in Washington Territory he could not gain enough support to win nomination for a third term in Congress. From the Republican administration he could hardly expect any appointment. Among Democrats, he had helped split the party and bring on the defeat of Douglas. When war came and the Union needed experienced military commanders, he volunteered his services and waited in vain for a commission. In the end he was made colonel of a demoralized regiment of New York volunteers.

He rose in rank to brigadier general, and after months of tedious duty in South Carolina he returned to lively action in northern Virginia. In September 1862 his daring, patriotism, and ambition blazed again in a final dramatic tableau. He was killed in a gallant charge, carrying the regimental colors directly against a heavy attack from the troops of Stonewall Jackson.

Looking back over his record, should one stress his high principles, intelligence, learning, and energy?[13] Or do they all pale against his relentless drive, which consumed even his own life in the end — the American flag in his hands and a bullet in his remarkable brain? Blink once at all that he dared and did and he looks like presidential timber. Blink again and he looks like scores of promising, somewhat distinguished young leaders of the mid-nineteenth century, straining to find a fitting place in a country that spanned a continent. Was Stevens a forceful, far-seeing, indispensable developer of the Northwest? Or was he a pushy little

---

13. Stevens's heroic death affected even his harshest critics, and in telling terms. Earlier we saw Ezra Meeker's charges that Stevens failed with Indians because he was drunk and deranged at the treaty councils. In context, Meeker uses alcoholism as a form of *extenuation* for Stevens's failures. He cannot otherwise explain how a man of such extraordinary competence and virtue could have done so much evil. Note that Meeker expresses Stevens's virtue as a willingness to break off old ties and risk his life for the great Union: "Words can but faintly portray the debt of gratitude the country owes the man, who, like, Stevens, severs his life-long political affiliation, cuts loose from all his old political associates, and in the darkest hour of our National existence throws himself into the breach to sacrifice his life that his country might live, as did Governor Stevens when he laid down his life on the bloody field of Chantilly, heroically struggling for the right" (Meeker, 58).

man with a head too big for his own good, risking everything out on the farthest reaches of United States territory — bringing law and ambition to the support of a few hundred settlers and doubtful benefits to a few thousand Indians?

This balance of questions may urge us to blink once more and recognize again the sharpness of Seattle's challenge. Stevens's career illustrates the promises of Young America propaganda. It fulfills the ideal of assimilating the West into both a vast self and a vast new republic. But it also illustrates how painful even a forceful drive to the West could be — how chancy and brief its moments of glory, and how personally destructive its code of impatient aggression.

From what we have seen of Stevens the ambitious and sometimes imperious commander, we might conclude that he was self-centered, hard, and cold. But his personal papers reveal a long record of family devotion and affection. As an American official, Stevens took possession of the land in his maps, reports, laws, and records. As an American settler, he also had plans for building a permanent home on the properties he could claim. He wrote about the land in that way, too, in meditations something like Hawthorne's. And he left a legacy of his own spirit there, especially in the life of his son.

Stevens kept up correspondence with many people who were dear to him. He wrote to his father for years, long after he had grown distant in outlook from that demanding and sometimes inflictive man. He often wrote to his wife; when duties called him away from her he would write something every day, sealing up a long journal letter when the chance finally emerged to transmit it safely. He wrote to friends. He wrote to relatives. Through this incidental habit he developed another kind of answer to the charge in Seattle's speech. He wove fine lines of connection across the map of his life. What he observed he wrote. What he wrote he shared. He thus made reports from West Point a part of his home back in Massachusetts and wrote up the scenes of Mexico to make them part of his home back in Newport, Rhode Island. He may have left the land of his fathers, seemingly without regret. But in steady practice he remained connected, warmly connected, to the scenes of his youth, his friendships, his marriage, and his growing family.

A single letter, now preserved at Yale, provides the full flavor of Stevens's longing for wide and deep family connections. It is addressed to Mrs. Benjamin Hazard, his mother-in-law, in Newport, Rhode Island, from some spot on the trail: "Camp on the Missouri —near Fort Benton, August 28th, 1855." Here Stevens was nearing the grandest council of his career, as he explains later in the letter: "We are doing famously with our Treaties. Soon we shall have assembled here Eight thousand Indians and the Blackfoot Treaty will we hope be made." (Weeks later, on October 22, he wrote again: "We have succeeded beyond our most sanguine expectations in establishing a peace between the Blackfeet Indians and the Indians of Washington.") But uppermost in his mind as he sat and scratched ink upon paper was a need to reach out to the widowed mother of his wife and make explicit the feelings of his heart.

"My dear Mother," he begins, and within a paragraph he becomes very frankly affectionate: "From having perhaps early lost my own mother, and for many years having had no sister living, I have felt a deep interest in the welfare and happiness of you and yours, and it has always seemed to me that the mother and sisters of Margaret were my own mother and sisters. I can hardly write as freely as usual in expressing my feelings at this time."[14] Despite this disclaimer, Stevens goes on to express feelings very well. He opens an intimate glimpse into his sense of time and change and the shell of stern duty that has grown over the domestic comforts he knew years before:

> How changed we are in a few years! I was when I was first married, scarcely any thing more than a dreamer, and not looking much beyond the day. How I then enjoyed your quiet family circle. It was the first family I had known since I was a child of 10 years where I really felt at home as I did in my own mother's house, before that mother died. I have now ceased to be a dreamer. The stern work of the times I have to do. Sometimes bright visions of the future illuminate the way. But never do I lose sight or forget that family circle or those old remembrances, the dearest, the fondest of my life. I write now, because I have time and there is occasion for it.

The immediate occasion seems to have been the wedding plans of his wife's younger sister. Stevens extends cordiality wide from coast to coast:

> There is no knowing what a day may bring forth. Tell Alfred and Nancy, that we will all meet I hope one of these days on the shores of Puget Sound, under my roof. Most joyously shall they be welcomed. We will try in a few years to *improve the communications.* They shall have a free Ticket when the cars first run from Lake

---

14. Isaac I. Stevens to Mrs. Benjamin Hazard, August 28, 1855, Beinecke Library, Yale University. The letter of October 22, 1855, is bound in the same volume: WA.MSS.S.192.

Superior to the Sound, and that time is not far distant. We shall still be young.

When he wrote these lines Stevens was thirty-seven. This paragraph reveals him still a sanguine dreamer, poignantly unaware of how long a railroad will actually be in coming or how soon war will cut off all his plans. Yet the next paragraph brings him back to practicalities, and back to touching the earth next to Puget Sound:

I can hardly look forward to any definite time, when we shall be able to revisit the States. A competency must be provided for my family. A farm has been started, which will afford a living, in case I do not continue in public life. My office continues for a little more than a year and a half longer. The duties of it will not be so arduous next year, as they have been, and I hope to be able to pass most of the time with Margaret and the children. I shall push the farm ahead, giving my personal attention to it. It will this year, from what I learn, be no loss, though I have to depend entirely for its management upon a friend.

So Stevens reports the results of almost two years in the West. He has acquired land, settled his family, planted crops, begun to break even, and turned his thoughts back to his distant relatives, lightly encouraging them to join him and "improve the communications." In his way, he would translate the dearest, fondest scenes of family life from Rhode Island to the rooms under his new roof in Washington Territory.

In just these paragraphs, Stevens implicates himself and all his kin in the act of settlement, dispossessing Indians to make space for the new homes and farms of immigrants from "the States." He expressly aims to replace the tribal associations of Indian generations in this landscape with the family associations of his generation. If we can count his mother-in-law, he would project his past generations into this new place as well. He has pushed Seattle and other Indians onto reservations, but now he will take up where they left off, to make the soil rich with the life of kindred — Stevens kindred.

Of course, such a rich family heritage could not be established in just a few years. As events turned out, Stevens returned to the East. He died in Virginia and was buried back in Rhode Island. But his family did come west to stay, after all. After the war they returned to the family property in Washington Territory, and it was there that the last of his children died in 1941. Most of his grandchildren were born on army posts in the West (Richards 391–92, 443 *n* 6). And in a dozen ways his one surviving son fulfilled the father's designs on the future. He followed his father's example, deeds, words, records, and maps. In fact, Hazard Stevens devoted much of his life to seeking and honoring his father's spirit in place after place on both sides of the continent.

The son fell wounded on the battlefield in Virginia, just minutes before his father ran ahead to lift the falling flag and meet his death. Hazard Stevens was then a captain. He recovered to become, at age twenty-three, the youngest general in the army, brevetted to brigadier's rank just before the end of the war. Many years later he was awarded the Congressional Medal of Honor. Isaac Stevens's modern biographer writes that Hazard "continued the Civil War career that his father was denied" and later followed his father's lead in many channels of ambition. He found government appointments at Olympia after the war; studied law (as his father had once planned to do); became an attorney for the North-

ern Pacific Railroad; became involved in the long boundary dispute over the San Juan Islands; and eventually ran for office
though he did not achieve a seat in Congress (Richards, 390–92).
He developed the family property in Olympia into a very advanced
model dairy farm up to the time of his death in 1918, though he,
too, was buried at last in Rhode Island.[15]

Hazard also traced his father's footsteps very deliberately at
least twice. He and another adventurer were the first to climb
Mount Rainier in 1870, and he labored to celebrate his father in a
thorough biography published in 1900. The mountain ascent re-
embodied his father's young daring in the West. The biography
looked back on the father's heroism and found it worthy of two
heavy volumes.

Mount Rainier is the highest point in Washington State, a four-
teen-thousand-foot landmark visible (on a clear day) throughout
the region that surrounds Puget Sound. Climbing it was a way of
claiming it, as Hazard knew. He proudly reported that he alone
had made the climb unscathed, outlasting "Edward T. Coleman,
an English gentleman of Victoria," who dropped out early, and P. B.
Van Trump, who was injured on the descent (Hazard Stevens,
"The Ascent," 513–14). Stevens thus misspells the name of
Edmund T. Coleman and suppresses his distinction as a rival British mountaineer. In 1868 Coleman had been part of the first group
to ascend Mount Baker, the highest volcanic peak in the north
Cascades. He had had earlier climbing experience in the Alps; he
sketched many scenes of the Mount Baker climb; and he wrote
that adventure up in a long, highly literary, and fully illustrated

---

15. Stevenson, 12–13. See also Stevens's obituaries in the *Morning
Olympian* (October 13 and 17, 1918). The farmhouse Hazard Stevens had
built still stands as a private residence in the neighborhood near Olympia
High School.

account in *Harper's* in 1869.[16] As Stevens recounts the ascent of Mount Rainier, however, he alone becomes the dauntless all-American adventurer. And we can see him repeating many of his father's experiences, to wrest this high point of Washington Territory from nature, from Indians, and even from guardian spirits at the summit.

Hazard's exploration re-enacts many of the adventures Isaac Stevens recorded on the way west during his railroad survey: problems with equipment, loss and malfunctioning of instruments, close calls with animals while crossing a swollen stream, attacks by swarms of mosquitoes, survival on short rations and local game, and days of unrelenting labor to make scant progress. Again there are passages of exclamation over unforeseen beauty in rugged and newly opened country. But most importantly, here again are encounters with long-time dwellers in this landscape, whose mastery of it first serves a Stevens and then passes into his superior grasp.

Hazard and his companions approached the mountain from the southwest, by a route up the Nisqually River Valley. Near Yelm

---

16. Coleman, 793–817. Coleman's article includes many descriptive passages about Puget Sound communities and the customs of local Indians, including their spiritual beliefs and their adaptation to life on reservations. Coleman also acknowledges that he and his companions were guided to their final base camp by "four trustworthy Indians" (794), and that it was these men's canoe skills that brought them back safe through whitewater rivers, "the most exciting portion of the whole journey" (815). It is only fair to add that Coleman did tire easily. Even on the Mount Baker ascent he says he had a hard time keeping up with younger climbers: "My sedentary life and the want of training told upon me, [and] twelve years absence from the Alps had not improved my pedestrian powers" (809).

Prairie, James Longmire supplied mules and a pack horse and led the mountaineers over a blind trail into country where only Indians camped. By good fortune, they came upon a small Indian family — a man named Sluiskin, his wife, and two small children. Sluiskin agreed to guide them to the base of the mountain. Later, he met the returning pair and helped with the rescue of Van Trump.

Sluiskin figures in this account as a living intermediary between the old ways of this formidable terrain and the past century of white invasion and settlement. He spoke Chinook Jargon, "that high-bred lingo invented by the old fur-traders," and he wore an outfit that was a curious composition of buckskin, fur, wild eagle feathers, and modern brass (Hazard Stevens, "Ascent," 519). He helped the mountaineers find their way to the snow fields, but then balked, warning that the mountain, after all, was a realm of potent spirits:

> Takhoma [Rainier], he said, was an enchanted mountain, inhabited by an evil spirit, who dwelt in a fiery lake on its summit. No human being could ascend it or even attempt its ascent, and survive. . . . Moreover, a furious tempest continually swept the crown of the mountain, and the luckless adventurer, even if he wonderfully escaped the perils below, would be torn from the mountain and whirled through the air by this fearful blast. And the awful being upon the summit, who would surely punish the sacrilegious attempt to invade his sanctuary, — who could hope to escape his vengeance? Many years ago, he continued, his grandfather, a great chief and warrior, and a mighty hunter, had ascended part way up the mountain, and had encountered some of these dangers, but he fortunately turned back in time to escape destruction; and no other Indian had ever gone so far. (522)

When Stevens and Van Trump rejected this appeal, Sluiskin begged for a note exonerating him from having a hand in their deaths. That night, he kept up "a most dismal chant, or dirge, until late in the night. The dim, white, spectral mass towering so near, the roar of the torrents below us, and the occasional thunder of avalanches, several of which fell during the night, added to the weird effect of Sluiskin's song." The next night, as if nature had joined in the warning, "the firs round our camp took fire and suddenly burst out in a vivid conflagration" (523).

Despite all these warnings and omens, Stevens and Van Trump pressed on. On the late afternoon of August 17, 1870, they waved their flags in triumph on the southwest peak, which is still called Point Success. A few hours later they reached the main summit, which turned out to be a ridge around a volcanic crater. They camped inside the crater for the night, frozen on one side and steam heated on the other. The next morning they left a brass plate in a cleft in a boulder, then hurried to descend before a storm could cut them off. Names on modern maps still commemorate them: Stevens Canyon, Van Trump Park, Sluiskin Falls.

From the features that the two mountaineers found at the top, we should perhaps question their originality. Had Indian people actually gone all the way to the top, to find the volcanic crater that corresponds to the "fiery lake" of Sluiskin's description? Or was that account based on long-transmitted tales of past volcanic activity? As Stevens found on the return trip, Sluiskin knew more than he was willing to tell. When forced to get help for Van Trump, he led the way back over a much shorter route and managed to find surprising short-cuts and obscure passages through thick timber.

Stevens came to admire Sluiskin as a man of high intelligence, "a shrewd, sarcastic wit," and fierce independence. He disdained to render allegiance to any tribe "and undoubtedly regarded the superintendent of Indian affairs, or even the great father at Washington himself, with equally contemptuous indifference" (530). But Stevens himself won this Indian's grudged respect. Sluiskin had called Coleman, the mountaineer who dropped behind, a "cultus [worthless] King George man" (520). But when he went back to rescue Van Trump, Sluiskin muttered a curse. He came again to the point where he had tried to mislead Stevens and had been forced to reveal a shorter way: "Skookum tenas man [powerful little man]," he said, "hiyu goddam" (529–30). A year later he brought mountain-sheep skins as friendly gifts to Stevens and Van Trump (527).

It is easy to see the conquest of Mount Rainier as a young man's exploit. Hazard Stevens was just twenty-eight in 1870, almost a decade younger than his *skookum tenas* father had been when he faced Indians in council and brought his son along as a witness. But facing hardship, conquering territory, and confronting Indians and Indian spirits were not enough to release Hazard from his father's domination. For at least another thirty years he would remain devoted to his father's spirit, assiduously retracing his story in all its details.

The biography of his father is hardly a work of even-handed scholarship. Kent Richards calls it a classic example of hagiography: "Hazard freely deleted injurious material, twisted facts, or, more usually, gave only one side of the story" (Richards, xiv, 450). But the flaws of the historian were the virtues of a proud descendent. In Hazard's memory, Isaac Stevens had been a mentor, a brave companion, and a fallen comrade and commander — a hero worth defending and celebrating in print. In the process of gathering materials and writing over a thousand pages, Hazard gave up years of his own life. We must suppose that, to explain military campaigns, geographical surveys, treaty councils, and political maneuvers, he sat patiently by the hour, retracing step by step with maps and journals open before him. He admits that he literally retraced many scenes. He went back to pace the Virginia battlefield at least twice after the war (Hazard Stevens, *Life* 2:496–97).

Meanwhile he continued to live within the confines of the world his father had explored. The biographer grew old with pen in hand. What must it have been to live always with the ghost of an excellent father peering over his shoulder? To travel back and forth from coast to coast, and see landmarks everywhere that the father had seen or even erected? To survive decade after decade and never find another full range of identity, as the father had done? To grow old, unmarried and childless, walking daily over the grounds the father had staked out near Olympia, seeing the tree trunks grow thicker and new generations of settlers coming with the railroad and crowding each other — until new international wars obliterated the importance of long-gone struggles for empire?

Isaac Stevens answered Seattle's speech one way in his life, with confident American patriotism, reinforcing a sense of dynamic progress, duty well done, and personal ambition in tune with Manifest Destiny. In death he answered again, through the long devotion he somehow inspired in the son he once brought west and carried along to see how treaties were made. For Hazard Stevens the prophecy of Seattle's speech was fulfilled in a strange way. Standing in Olympia or almost anywhere, he would know, even if he never heard the words, that "when your children's children shall think themselves alone in the field, the store, the shop, upon the highway or the silence of the woods they will not be alone." His own father would be there among the "hosts that once filled and still love this beautiful land." And for the Stevenses this beautiful land was not limited to one city or one region but embraced the entire continent.

CHAPTER 6

Remembered Places,
Remembered Voices

AT THIS POINT it may seem that the answers to Seattle's speech are overwhelming. It may be a touching speech of protest, but the world it addressed was prepared to cut it down, or, worse, absorb it into the massive lore of continental America. Political leaders were thoroughly primed to ignore such speeches or set them aside as ineffectual curiosities. Attentive listeners such as Stevens or Gibbs were prepared to hear Indians one way as cultural informants and quite another as political representatives. Even Dr. Smith, who published the text we have, could hold it with a very strange grasp, heralding it one week as the relic of a magnificint orator, undercutting it the next as the rattle of a "sable" old "Cicero of the Sound."

But as we noted at the beginning of this study, the speech as we have it presents a deep and abiding challenge to our loyalties and predilections. As readers, we run a risk of literate prejudice ourselves. Because there is a wealth of surviving written and printed material with which to document the life of Isaac Stevens or Thomas Jefferson, we may simply assume that they were essentially larger or more comprehensive — in a word, wiser — than people like Seattle, who inhabited a world of myth, legend, and oratory.

The speech directly attacks this easy assumption. This is the final turn of the screw of the puzzle it presents. As readers and critics, we have to recognize that Indian oratory fits a well-worn literary pattern. It even fits a cultural stereotype. But that is not the only pattern that adequately describes it. Taken on its own terms, this speech claims to speak for the land, speak beyond a particular occasion, and speak for spirits that will endure. In very obvious ways, it continues to do all these things. Although it is not a single, unified, coherent record, it is still a powerful symbol. It may envelop some actual words of Seattle or other Indians. It continues to strike chords of recognition among some groups of Indians, and of guilt among successors of white invaders.[1] By having attained worldwide fame, however fortuitously, it still towers over the largely forgotten careers of Stevens and his contemporaries.

Does Seattle thus persist in answering his answerers? To weigh this possibility we need to look at two further backgrounds to this speech: persisting features of geography in and around the city of Seattle, and persisting records of indigenous beliefs.

The legend of Chief Seattle still holds a particular meaning in the Puget Sound region, especially around the city of Seattle. For those who have spent any time there, what the speech says rings true to an obvious fact about that geography. Seattle has grown and grown. Houses have spread over its hills, tall buildings have gone straight up from the central core, and great derricks handle

---

1. Recent developments include a bestselling children's book, *Brother Eagle, Sister Sky* (1991), based on a much-revised version of Perry's text; and "Circle of Faith — The Words of Chief Seattle" (1992), a musical composition by James VanDemark, based on Smith's text. The children's book has the subtitle *A Message from Chief Seattle*, but, except for a small figure on the title page, its illustrations show Plains and Eastern Woodland Indians on horseback and in birchbark canoes. See Fruchter for a description of the VanDemark work, which has been performed around the country by the Muir Quartet and an American Indian drum group.

the cargoes of huge container ships in the port. But natural features around the city continue to dwarf these man-made impositions. The Cascade Range hovers in the distance to the east. Mount Rainier floats above the clouds morning and evening through all seasons of the year. The sun goes down behind the Olympic Mountains to the west — beyond Puget Sound and its islands. The city sits on steep hills around a bay, between salt water to the west and long Lake Washington to the east, with Lake Union and a ship canal in between. Almost anywhere in the city a person can walk just around a corner or over a few blocks and see a large scene of trees, water, hills, and mountains. Thousands of people keep boats and use them year round in the mild climate, even when their neighbors put ski racks on the car and head into the mountains. Within an hour or two it is possible still to get far from urban life — into a forest, onto a broad stretch of water, out to the rough coastline of the Pacific. Many commute into the city by ferry and watch the city recede and grow small again under the shoulders of its hills every late afternoon.

The contours of the land seem to remain as the first inhabitants knew them, and to assert their presence so that citified sophistication often seems silly in Seattle. If people remember the bright lights of this city, it is because they shine in regular lines over hill upon hill, except in the quiet open spaces of water, where a bridge twinkles quietly or a ferry cuts a track patiently through the dark. And the ferries — most of them with Indian or Chinook Jargon names such as *Quinault, Illahee,* and *Klahowya* — slide into the heart of town only to slide back out again and cross the Sound.

A sense persists that city and wilderness are almost in touch with each other. Of course that is a comforting illusion. In fact the weekend fisherman, beachcomber, or mountaineer from Seattle is likely to have very sophisticated work through the week. The city's prosperity has always developed in tight unison with advances in technology, especially the kinds of technology that refigure space and time. It was for ports to the Orient that Puget Sound was first explored by European and American navigators in the age of sail. The city developed through the nineteenth century as a port for steam vessels and a steam railroad terminus. With airplanes came the Boeing Company, and the development of long range propeller and jet aircraft. The B-29, B-52, and 747 all are proud achievements of Seattle-based designers and workers. In recent decades both the world and the local economy have been transformed by the development of personal computers, with software pioneered by local companies. Within a little over a century the distance between Seattle and New York or Tokyo has been reduced from weeks to hours to fractions of a second. And at each stage, this region has been particularly involved in global change.

Such developments have a dark side that should be acknowledged, too. The area that Stevens came to survey as Washington Territory now holds large tracts of land still under federal jurisdiction. There are considerable areas marked off as Indian reservations and national parks and forests. But there are also unapproachable military reservations and nuclear sites. By the ingenuity of modern Americans, some tracts of the state have been altered for centuries to come. Forests have been clear-cut. Fisheries have been choked off by huge hydroelectric dams. The tiny villages of the pioneers have been paved over and exploited for the needs of recent millions.

Modern Seattle thus embraces a conflict between overwhelming powers. The grandeur of ocean, mountains, and evergreen nature can be glimpsed just around the corner if not right outside the windows. But every hour jet aircraft pass overhead and quickly climb above Mount Rainier. All night the central streets and buildings pulse with intelligently programmed electrons.

Is there anywhere left in this setting for the tribal, close-knit affection for the land that Seattle's speech promises? Or can there still be a meaningful trace of what the Stevenses and other early white settlers tried to establish, in their turn? Other answers to Chief Seattle emerge if we look at two of the oldest areas of the city and the symbols they still preserve from the past.

West Seattle is a neighborhood cut off from the rest of the city and particularly marked with mementos of the Indian past. The district is a wide peninsula between the Duwamish River and Puget Sound, with a point jutting north into the main Seattle harbor, Elliott Bay. Seattle and his people came to fish at the mouth of the Duwamish. It was on these shores that some of the first white settlers landed in 1851. School children (including my own fourth-grade class) walked down from the top of the hill to witness a re-enactment a century later. A main route out from the city crosses Harbor Island and then climbs to the northwest along a high hill. At the top of the climb is Belvedere Viewpoint, a park that slopes down to the roadway and a wide parking area. From there, one looks across the entire harbor to the heart of the city. For years there has been a totem pole marking the edge of the vista. Since 1991 there has also been an explanatory marker quoting paragraphs from Chief Seattle's speech. West Seattle may seem to pride itself on its Indian background. The neighborhood summer festival is the Hi-Yu (Chinook Jargon for "plenty"). West Seattle High School, at the top of the hill, still has teams called the Indians, a newspaper called the *Chinook*, and a yearbook called the *Kimtah* (Afterwards). "Who are we? You should know. / West Seattle Indians, that's who!" So the school's fight song begins.

Recent nervousness about Indian symbols has run smack against the line that comes next: "Sing we proudly, our good name."[2]

By a quirk of city planning the school was built to face Stevens Street — named for the governor. Few Indians or descendants of Indians have lived in this neighborhood or attended its schools. Duwamish Indians once tried to develop an enclave above the river, but other West Seattle settlers burned them out of their homes in the 1890s (Ruby and Brown, 73). At Belvedere Viewpoint another new marker takes a long view of Puget Sound, from the time of the glaciers to the present, and celebrates the gathering of other peoples here "with heritages that spanned the globe: from *Europe* to *Asia*; from *Iceland* to the *Americas*; from *Africa* to *Australia* and the *Pacific Islands*."[3] Indian words and a few tokens remain, but they have been overwhelmed by decades of development by Europeans, Asians, Africans, and their descendants. Some residents are now in their fourth and fifth generations here, but many more are newcomers with little more than faint school-learning about Chief Seattle or Isaac Stevens or anything that would touch any deep resonance of local history. In fact the masthead of the *Chinook* newspaper carries as its Indian figure not a Puget Sound Indian but a Plains chief with a full headdress of eagle feathers. The high school used to distribute protective book covers showing an utterly grotesque Indian warrior, bare chested,

---

2. There is also a Sealth High School in the southern part of West Seattle. Its teams are called the Seahawks; its newspaper, the *Southwester*; its yearbook, the *Cache*. Chief Seattle was already celebrated by students when there was just one city high school, Seattle High School. Its first yearbook, called the *Sealth*, opened with an editorial honoring "Chief Sealth" (Seattle High School).

3. The current marker at Belvedere Viewpoint is credited to Dan Portman and dated 1991.

brandishing a tomahawk. The nearby park, where the school has its athletic fields, is named for an Indian out of Longfellow's poetry: Hiawatha Playfield.

The first white settlers at Alki left within a few months and moved to a more promising area across Elliott Bay. They filed their Donation Claims for lands that are now at the center of the city. And there, too, one can find long enduring monuments to the past. Pioneer Square is a triangle of land at First Avenue and Yesler, at the meeting point of the earliest claims. The Dennys and Borens took acres to the north. Doc Maynard filed his claim to the south. And when Henry Yesler came on the scene, they each yielded a little to him to open the skid road to his sawmill on the harborfront. The streets north of Yesler Way still run roughly northwest-southeast to parallel the old shoreline. Those south of Yesler run north-south, and do not quite match their counterparts. Hence the little triangle at their meeting point. And hence a deeper jaggedness in Seattle history.

There are monuments of Indians — a tall totem pole, a bust of Chief Seattle (with a drinking fountain at its back) — that have endured through decades of change around the adjoining streets. Trolleys have disappeared, leaving an iron pergola shelter as a quaint relic. Stone buildings put up after the great fire of 1889, having descended from glory to slum, are now revitalized as new shops, restaurants, and offices. Today tourists gather at Pioneer Square to begin walking tours or to hunt for bargains or souvenirs. Nearby are antique dealers, coffee shops and bookstores, a National Historical Park to commemorate the Alaska gold rush, and plush offices of law firms and trading companies. But traces of the skid road remain, too: missions and cheap hotels; panhandlers; bodies slumped near doorways or sagging in shabby clothes on ledges and benches. For decades this area has been a haunt of

Indians, living Indians, some of them descendants of Seattle's oldest people, neither assimilated nor confined to any reservation. Simply there.

Chief Seattle, after all, was involved in two different family groups. When he agreed to the Port Elliott Treaty, he made his mark to represent both the Duwamish and the Suquamish. He was a leader acknowledged by the Suquamish, his father's people, and he moved with them back to a huge ancestral lodge across Puget Sound for the rest of his life. The Duwamish, his mother's people, could not fit into life on that reservation. Most of them drifted back to the Duwamish River area after 1856. Some eventually found a place on the Muckleshoot Reservation near Auburn. But as years passed, the Duwamish tribe became a people with no fixed homeland, at least none recognized by the federal government.[4]

Meanwhile, Indians continued to trade and visit in the growing settlement on Elliott Bay. Chief Seattle was a well-known figure on the waterfront. So was his daughter, called Princess Angeline by some of the early settlers. Governor Stevens's earliest reports had noted the intractable attachment of local Indians to their accustomed places. They also remarked that these Indians could be useful where they were. In one passage Stevens repeated the word

---

4. The place of Duwamish Indians in Seattle has been complicated by many historical changes. By refusing to settle on established reservations, they lost claims to land and treaty rights. By assimilating or simply living in the Seattle area, they have sometimes come into uneasy alliances or disputes with other Indians, including Alaskan Indians, who have also settled in Seattle after losing hope or support elsewhere. See State of Washington Indian Affairs Task Force, esp. 87, 101–2, for some ramifications of these problems.

three times: "They are very useful in many ways, for transporting persons about the sound in their canoes, &c. Many of the men, as laborers, are very useful in chopping wood, plowing, driving wagons, &c. Some of the women wash clothes well, and in a variety of ways make themselves useful" (Isaac I. Stevens to George W. Manypenny, Dec. 26, 1853, p. 8). Despite Indian wars and the treaty stipulations about removal to reservations, Indian laborers went on working for low wages at Yesler's mill and living nearby. Small bands went on with their fishing, and carried passengers in their canoes. Angeline found her niche in Seattle, selling clams, washing clothes, and doing other domestic work from kitchen to kitchen. She died there in 1896 and was buried in Lakeview Cemetery.[5]

Clarence Bagley records that Indian shacks lined the Seattle waterfront in early years, including dingy gambling dens and sweat-houses (*History*, 1:96–98). But the lives of local Indians were not necessarily squalid, nor were white settlers always uneasy with Indians nearby. Early reminiscences report the comfort of having neighbors with ready canoes at hand, when the Duwamish River suddenly flooded. Indians also showed up with welcome fish and produce. When the first white twins were born, Indians saw them as a prodigy, and brought fish oil "with which the babies were rubbed for nourishment."[6] Chief Seattle was a famous and

---

5. Bagley, "Chief Seattle and Angeline," 269–75, includes many anecdotes about Angeline and part of a poem composed at her death. This article enlarges Bagley's earlier account in his *History of Seattle*, 1:83.

6. See *The Duwamish Diary, 1849–1949*, 80, 19. This book is a collection of local clippings and reminiscences about Duwamish Valley pioneers, compiled by the Laboratory Writing classes at Cleveland High School between 1947 and 1949.

welcome guest at great gatherings and celebrations. The Maples, a family of Duwamish settlers, threw an enormous party early in 1866:

> The greatest of all our greetings came when Chief Seattle, (Sealth), with his skin and furbedecked war canoe, with its fifty paddlers came round the bend and sang one of their songs of friendship upon landing in front of the house on the bank of the Duwamish River. He stepped out and became the sire and marshall of a tribe of savages, and with all the salaam that he could muster wished us happiness and joy at the festivity. Then he had his braves bring to us the skins of cougar and mink, some moccasins and some fish and salmon eggs, and with them offered us his good will and hearty cheer.[7]

But as a city grew up over a simple lumber mill and settlement, the survival of local Indians became ever more precarious. The Duwamish lost their lands and even their waterways. Major engineering projects rerouted the Duwamish River. The tidelands of Elliott Bay were filled in and platted for industrial development. A ship canal was built to connect Lake Washington with Puget Sound; it lowered the lake and wiped out its old outlets, little rivers that had fed into the Duwamish. Railroads and railroad yards moved in over areas once traversed by canoes.

Different ways of seeing the same space were well worn in this

---

7. Mary Ann (Maple) Cavanaugh, "Story of a Pioneer Party in King County Forty Years ago," *Seattle Post-Intelligencer* (January 21, 1906), quoted in *The Duwamish Diary*, 25. At the 1862 wedding of Henry Van Asselt and another Maple daughter, Chief Seattle and seven hundred followers are reported to have attended and set up a tremendous show (*The Duwamish Diary*, 11–12).

setting—and in the wider world—by 1900. They were implicit in the records of Isaac Stevens, and of Lewis and Clark—all of whom came west to incorporate the "savage" world beyond the Rockies into the maps of "civilized" science. They were implicit in 1792, when Captain Vancouver first sailed into Puget Sound, recording bearings and landmarks for the claims of far-flung empire. Some accounts of Chief Seattle suggest that as a small boy he sighted or even came aboard Vancouver's ship.[8] Indeed this same contrast— between lives shaped by one region and lives of world-encircling power—can be traced back through centuries. How did Columbus appear, we may wonder, to the peoples who sighted his ships in the Western Hemisphere, or, for that matter, to the settled European peoples who watched him depart? Or what of Mediterranean villagers who chanced to look up from their daily rhythms to see Herodotus, Alexander, or Caesar on the move?

Chief Seattle's speech finally holds our attention because it addresses this age-old contrast: "Your God loves your people and hates mine. . . . The ashes of our ancestors are sacred and their final resting place is hallowed ground, while you wander away from the tombs of your fathers seemingly without regret." The speech precisely challenges the cold difference between tribal values and the strange rootlessness of any empire builder. Yet it also attempts to reach across this conflict. It is a speech, after all, an act of hu-

---

8. Watt, 178; Anderson, 27–34. Anderson cites J. A. Castello, *The Siwash: Their Life, Legends, and Tales* (Seattle: The Calvert Co., 1895) and oral legends of the Suquamish people. Captain Vancouver's journal for May 20–24, 1792, simply records bartering sessions with Indians whose canoes came near his ship and a brief visit aboard the ship by two unnamed adult leaders.

man communication, an effort at conciliation, agreement, what we still call a meeting on common ground. As we know it, it is a speech recorded in English — a hybrid of indigenous speech and modern print culture. It seems somehow to connect these incommensurate realms.

In the end, we may learn most from this speech if we consider it as, frankly, one among many such efforts at connection. It is even rather odd as an oral performance among the many that have been recorded from this region. Just as Chief Seattle did not immediately fade from the scene in the 1850s and his people did not in fact disappear, so voices of Indians have kept on repeating well-worn stories from the past, thereby preserving living traces of Seattle's world down to the present. And decade after decade, more broadly sympathetic listeners have turned up to pursue such speech, to record it and appreciate its structures and implications.

Henry Smith's report of Seattle is maddeningly tantalizing largely because we have learned, since his time, to listen better. He gives just hints of exactly where and when he took down whatever he did. He fails to specify just how much he heard, in what language, and where he patched together phrases or passages of his own.

Many later students have taken better pains in recording scores of traditional stories and informal narratives. They have learned Indian languages and developed long acquaintanceships with their informants. Finally they have looked back at their notes and studies not with a momentary pang of nostalgia or celebration, but with enduring respect for the ways of another people. In other words, the legendary tableau of a towering Indian speaking out to indifferent treaty makers has been altered over time. As Indians have gone on talking, some new listeners have brought literacy to the aid of better attentiveness. The result is a large collection of records, and sometimes a different tableau, of a patient storyteller exchanging his (or very often her) recollections with an alert student through months or years of enlarged understanding.

The results have not always been so ideal, to put it mildly. But a depth of understanding has emerged here and there, enough to reveal some outlines of a large and complex Indian literature. We can now see just enough to know that the Seattle speech, taken alone, misrepresents the riches that his people carried in the stories they told.

A sobering starting point for Northwest oral literature is Melville Jacobs's 1962 article about the situation in Oregon. After decades of skilled and tireless collecting, Jacobs reported his life work with a heavy heart (Jacobs, 90–99). By the 1930s most Indian languages in Oregon were either extinct or represented by only a very few surviving speakers. Anthropologists had collected many stories in the Northwest, but seldom with the care they deserved. The records remained in obscure publications or unpublished notes, in a form that few students of literature could find appealing or even intelligible. What had been a lively cultural heritage — part of dances, ceremonies, art, and child-rearing — was crumbling to dust. Jacobs estimated that over 95 percent of the material that had been available in the nineteenth century was gone beyond recovery, and that "the sampling which has survived is not trustworthily representative" (95). Finally, he pronounced a discouraging warning about reading even that sample:

> It must be understood that stark translations of non-Western literatures permit only culture-bound perceptions. No matter how magnificently linguists have transcribed and translated such literatures, they are largely unintelligible, both in what they express

and in manner of expression, if nothing more than texts and translations are submitted to posterity. In such spare garb they must remain mostly meaningless, except to linguists, for all time to come. Unless each text is speedily supplemented by extensive sociocultural commentary compiled with the aid of the last inheritors of the culture, it remains worthless as a literary document, a tantalizing morsel which cannot really be reached. (97)

In the face of such gloom, however, a few hardy students have managed to make a varied sample of Northwest tales and speeches widely available. Compilations by Ella E. Clark (*Indian Legends of the Pacific Northwest*) and Jarold Ramsey (*Coyote Was Going There*) can be found in public libraries and bookstores throughout the region. Some of these stories have been revived through close analysis and expert discussion. Ramsey's series of essays, *Reading the Fire*, for example, provides a splendid introduction to this literature. Ramsey applies the skills of a Shakespeare scholar to several stories he admires, showing beyond dispute that the people of the Northwest had a developed and intricate oral culture long before they encountered Europeans — and long after.

Against this background, the speech of Chief Seattle begins to look like a forced and very unrepresentative performance. As a great public speech, a plangent farewell, addressed to an audience of white settlers and officials, it is a far cry from the intimate, often deeply humorous tales and legends and recollections that have come to light.

Finally, we can approach it from yet another angle, by turning to recollections more recent and approximate. In the 1930s, a young anthropologist named William Elmendorf collected stories among the Twana people of Puget Sound. Their reservation lies on the shores of Hood Canal, west of Seattle but adjacent to the regions Seattle knew and Governor Stevens surveyed. Elmendorf developed a friendship with two Twana men, Henry Allen and his older brother Frank. The older man was at first very hostile to white people, but Elmendorf had learned his language and eventually broke down his reserve. In time, he was able to take down eighty separate stories and recollections from these men, a rich mine of local history including stories from times contemporary with Chief Seattle and even earlier (Elmendorf, *Twana Narratives*).

Frank Allen was already in his seventies when Elmendorf first met him. He was over eighty in the summer of 1940, when he told his stories in long daily sessions (xxxiii). As the stories unfolded, both brothers revealed a number of connections they had to families and different language groups around Puget Sound. Both were old enough to remember important historical changes as part of their personal experience. But the older man remained "almost a holdover from the pre-reservation generation. . . . He seems to have been the last surviving Twana secret-society initiate, the last to have sponsored a native marriage feast, and the last to have given an adult's name-assuming feast" (xxxiv). His stories ranged from the mythic world of prehistory down to very recent happenings in the twentieth century. Most importantly, dozens of them relate to the acquisition and management of spirit power or "tamánamis" (as Elmendorf spells it). According to another informant, Frank Allen was widely known as a powerful shaman or spiritual doctor (xlvii). His stories reflect his constant involvement in realms of both the dead and the living, between the mythic past and the historical present. As Elmendorf interprets this material, the oral accounts given by these Twana men defy any simple separation of myth and history: "The literature of these people, unwritten and actualized only in recitation, existed on a myth-to-history continuum.... My hope is that this analysis may reveal something, if only a hint, about the thought world of Twana Indians of a century and a half ago" (liv).

For our purposes, these stories provide two kinds of hints or sidelights about Chief Seattle and his family. On the one hand, Frank Allen tells of Seattle's widely reported involvement in protecting the white settlements during the Indian Wars; he repeats the historical story that Seattle sent an admonition to Leschi, which spared the town of Seattle from an attack (154). But on the other hand, he tells of raids between the Chemakum and the Suquamish, in which Seattle's son was killed by a mysterious bullet that was fated to hit him twice (143–44); and he describes Moses Seattle, the chief's grandson born around 1900, as a child brought back from the land of the dead: "He grew up, but he was funny. He had no bones" (232).

The Allens' many stories of spirit powers make it clear that this is a very complex subject, hardly explicable after a century. Puget Sound Indians knew and sometimes controlled an array of powers, which they encountered through mysterious and secret means. Elmendorf reports his own reluctance to press Henry Allen personally on this point (xxxv), but the stories themselves freely mention cures, visits to the realm of the dead, war powers, wealth powers, shamanism, soul loss and recovery, love and hate magic, and various rituals. Some passages stress the special fame of Seattle's Duwamish people for their ritual visits to the land of the dead (237) — a point reinforced in other studies.[9] Many pas-

---

9. Several earlier accounts are brought together and enlarged in T. T. Waterman, "The Paraphernalia of the Duwamish 'Spirit Canoe' Ceremony."

sages repeat the term "tamánamis" in such varied ways that it seems impossible to pin it down without a firm and detailed narrative context.

As a result, the mention of *tahmanawis* in the Seattle speech seems to flash more clearly for a moment and then lapse into obscurity. The word could refer to a particular funeral ceremony, a visit to the land of the dead to confirm that someone recently dead had indeed arrived there. This use of the Duwamish ceremony has in fact been described in some detail by T. T. Waterman (Waterman, 137). But the term as the Allens use it could just as easily refer to any of dozens of manifestations of spirit power and ritual practices.

In a longer view, the Allens' narratives should remind us yet again that the realm of oral history and ceremonial may be impossible to translate into cold prose publication. The Allens preserve their memories of Seattle in casual remarks; they mention him as a chief, a warrior, a man involved like themselves in spiritual events season after season. But unlike the Seattle speech, their stories reveal depths by indirection. One story leads to another and another. One day's talk leads the teller to keep "dredging" his memory and take a new direction when he meets the listener the next day (Elmendorf, *Twana Narratives*, xlvi–xlvii). What endured into the 1990s, when Elmendorf finally published *Twana Narratives*, was thus the recollection of Seattle in living voices — not his own, but those of other men who evidently knew his language and his ways, and could trust a white researcher enough to keep talking.

The Seattle speech may seem spurious, for all its fame, a strange document that never actually fulfilled all that it might promise.

Who heard or read it, and went on to heed it? Isaac Stevens, who should have paid close attention, has left no record of such a speech. Certainly it never delayed his course in pressing Seattle to sign a treaty. No one else kept any record to corroborate in detail the account Henry Smith printed decades later. As for Smith, he wrote out plaintive paragraph after paragraph. But in his other writings he ignored them. His very next installment of reminiscences turned Seattle into a mere name, an awkward rhyme. Smith's long career involved buying up what had been Indian lands and growing rich, apparently without remorse.

Seattle himself, by all accounts, remained a fast friend to the new settlement, with never another whisper of mordant irony in any speech. His people did not mournfully disappear, as the speech foretold. They came back to their shorelines for many decades; some dwell there even now. Yet land development has gone on ruthlessly in the Duwamish Valley and from Puget Sound right up the slopes of the Cascades. New generations have come and produced their own children and grandchildren. Remaining symbols and public tokens of indigenous peoples are faintly understood, if noticed at all.

Finally, the famous speech has itself been rewritten, mutilated, and rehashed beyond recognition to attain its current renown. Even the most sympathetic reader can misread it easily — as a touching speech, perhaps, but a statement that *can* be fully understood (and smugly assimilated) by a patient reader.

In the end, after all that we have now seen, this composition defies such resolution. It seems impossible to unfold its origins, explain its mysteries, or fit it into any satisfactory coherence with the other speeches of the Indian called Seattle, or with the other writings of Henry Smith, or with the other documents of early history on Puget Sound. The speech asks hard questions, and leaves them unanswered in a disturbing void. Other American thinkers — as formidable as Jefferson, Whitman, and Hawthorne — have pondered and even shaped answers to these same questions. Other American spirits — as forceful as Isaac Stevens and the builders of modern industrial empires — have met them head-on with their dedicated lives. But the questions do not go away, even so. Why must a well-tried pattern of life give way utterly to another, even in a place of resources in abundance? How does anyone, in our time, grow into a homeland? And when a homeland can be lightly swept away, what will endure?

By asking these questions, and by leaving them unresolved, this speech may properly disturb the world from which it has sprung. Like the earthquakes and volcanic eruptions that shake the West Coast from time to time, and always seem poised to shake much harder, it can serve as a healthy reminder. Living, as all Americans do, where Indians lived not very long ago, we could do well to remember that everyone living is passing. What we think of as established civilization is not inevitable, nor necessarily the best arrangement for any region. And what will last may not be what we think will last. The Seattle speech may not be "authentic" — the words of one Indian that just one hearer managed somehow to transcribe accurately. Even if it were, it would not be an adequate expression of early voices and spirits in the Far West. But it points us toward those voices and toward many other mysteries that survived there long after Seattle seemed to say farewell.

REFERENCES

Addison, Joseph, and Richard Steele. *The Spectator*, edited by Donald F. Bond. 5 vols. Oxford: Clarendon Press, 1965.

Amoss, Pamela. *Coast Salish Spirit Dancing: The Survival of an Ancient Religion*. Seattle: University of Washington Press, 1978.

Anderson, Eva Greenslit. *Chief Seattle*. Caldwell, Id.: Caxton Printers, 1943.

Arrowsmith, William. "Speech of Chief Seattle, January 9, 1855." *Arion* 8 (1969): 461–64.

———. "Indian Speeches and the Deathsong of Red Bird." *American Poetry Review* 2 (January/February 1973): 10–11.

Bagley, Clarence B. "Chief Seattle and Angeline." *Washington Historical Quarterly* 22 (1931): 243–75.

———. *History of Seattle: From the Earliest Settlement to the Present Time*. 3 vols. Chicago: S. J. Clarke, 1916.

Beckham, Stephen Dow. "George Gibbs, 1815–1873: Historian and Ethnologist." Ph.D. diss., University of California at Los Angeles, 1969.

Binns, Archie. *Northwest Gateway: The Story of the Port of Seattle*. New York: Doubleday, 1941.

Brasher, Thomas L. *Whitman as Editor of the Brooklyn Daily Eagle*. Detroit: Wayne State University Press, 1970.

Brown, Richard Maxwell. "Language and Exploration: The Role of the Chinook Jargon." In *Encounters with a Distant Land: Exploration and the Great Northwest*, edited by Carlos Schwantes. Moscow, Id.: University of Idaho Press, 1994.

Buerge, David. "Hail to the Chief." *Seattle Weekly* (September 1, 1993), 19–27.

———. "The Man We Call Seattle." *Seattle Weekly* (June 29, 1983), 24–27.

———. "Seattle's King Arthur." *Seattle Weekly* (July 17, 1991), 27–29.

———, ed. *Chief Seattle*. Seattle: Sasquatch Books, 1992.

Campbell, Joseph, with Bill Moyers. *The Power of Myth*. New York: Doubleday, 1988.

Clark, Ella E. "George Gibbs' Account of Indian Mythology in Oregon and Washington Territories." *Oregon Historical Quarterly* 56 (1955): 293–325, and 57 (1956): 125–67.

———, ed. *Indian Legends of the Pacific Northwest*. Berkeley and Los Angeles: University of California Press, 1953.

Clark, Jerry L. "Thus Spoke Chief Seattle: The Story of an Undocumented Speech." *Prologue* 17 (Spring 1985): 58–65.

Cohen, Fay G. *Treaties on Trial: The Continuing Controversy over Northwest Indian Fishing Rights*. Seattle: University of Washington Press, 1986.

Coleman, Edmund T. "Mountaineering on the Pacific." *Harper's* 39 (1869): 793–817.

Coues, Elliott, ed. *History of the Expedition under the Command of Lewis and Clark*. 3 vols. 1893. Reprint, New York: Dover, 1965.

Curti, Merle. "Young America." *American Historical Review* 32 (1926/27): 34–55.

Deloria, Vine, Jr. *God is Red: A Native View of Religion*. 2d ed. Golden, Colo.: Fulcrum, 1994.

Documents Relating to the Negotiations of Ratified and Unratified Treaties with Various Indian Tribes, 1801–1869. National Archives And Records Administration Microfilm Publication T494.

Donaldson, Thomas. *The Public Domain: Its History, with Statistics*. U.S. Congress. House. 46th Congress, 3rd sess., 1881. Executive document 47, part 4.

The Duwamish Diary, 1849-1949. Seattle: Cleveland High School, 1949.

Eastman, Arthur, et al., eds. *The Norton Reader*, shorter 8th ed. New York: Norton, 1992.

Eby, Edwin Harold. *A Concordance of Walt Whitman's Leaves of Grass and Selected Prose Writings*. 5 parts. Seattle: University of Washington Press, 1949–54.

Eells, Myron. *The Indians of Puget Sound: The Notebooks of Myron Eells.* Edited by George Pierre Castile. Seattle: University of Washington Press, 1985.

Elmendorf, William W. *The Structure of Twana Culture.* Washington State University Research Studies 28, No. 3, supplement (1960).

———. *Twana Narratives: Native Historical Accounts of a Coast Salish Culture.* Seattle: University of Washington Press, 1993.

Emerson, Ralph Waldo. *Ralph Waldo Emerson: Essays and Lectures.* Edited by Joel Porte. New York: Library of America, 1983.

Fruchter, Rena. "2 Groups Give Voice to an Indian Chief's Words." *New York Times* (September 19, 1993), sec. 3, p. 9.

Gibbs, George. Journal of George Gibbs. National Archives and Records Administration, Records group 76.

———. "Notes from Mr. Gibbs regarding Expedition to arrest the Murderers of Young." National Archives Microfilm Publication M5, roll 23.

Goetzmann, William H. *Army Exploration in the American West 1803–1863.* New Haven: Yale University Press, 1959.

Grant, Frederick James. *History of Seattle, Washington.* New York: American Publishing and Engraving Co., 1891.

Hawthorne, Nathaniel. *The Scarlet Letter and Selected Tales.* Edited by Thomas E. Connolly. Harmondsworth: Penguin, 1970.

Hodge, Frederick Webb, ed. *Handbook of American Indians North of Mexico.* Smithsonian Institution, Bureau of American ethnology, Bulletin 30. 1905. 2 vols. Reprint, New York: Pageant Books, 1959.

Jacobs, Melville. "The Fate of Indian Oral Literatures in Oregon." *Northwest Review* 5 (1962): 90–99.

Jeffers, Susan, illus. *Brother Eagle, Sister Sky: A Message from Chief Seattle.* New York: Dial Books, 1991.

Jefferson, Thomas. *Notes on the State of Virginia.* Edited by William Peden. 1954. Reprint, New York: Norton, 1972.

Joseph, Chief. "An Indian's View of Indian Affairs." *North American Review* 128 (1879): 415–33.

Kaiser, Rudolph. "Chief Seattle's Speech(es): American Origins and European Reception." In *Recovering the Word: Essays on Native American Literature*, edited by Brian Swann and Arnold Krupat, 497–536. Berkeley and Los Angeles: University of California Press, 1987.

Krenmayr, Janice. "'The Earth Is Our Mother': Who Really Said That?" *Seattle Times Sunday Magazine* (January 5, 1975), 4–6.

Lauter, Paul, et al., eds. *The Heath Anthology of American Literature*. 2 vols. Boston: D.C. Heath, 1990.

Lawrence, D.H. *Studies in Classic American Literature*. 1924. Reprint, Harmondsworth: Penguin, 1971.

Lee, W. Storrs, ed. *Washington State: A Literary Chronicle*. New York: Funk & Wagnalls, 1969.

LeWarne, Charles P. *Washington State*. Seattle: University of Washington Press, 1986.

Manypenny, George W. Report of the Commissioner of Indian Affairs. In U.S. House, Executive Document 1, 33rd Congress, 2d session (1854), part 1, 211–544.

McDonald, Lucile. "Hard Work Lines Pocket With Cash." *Seattle Times*, Charmed Land Magazine section (April 23, 1963), 6.

———. "Pioneer Doctor with Advanced Ideas." *Seattle Times Sunday Magazine* (January 24, 1960), 3.

McQuade, Donald, et al. eds. *The Harper American Literature*. 2d ed. 2 vols. New York: Harper Collins, 1993.

Meeker, Ezra. *The Tragedy of Leschi*. 1905. Reprint, Seattle: Historical Society of Seattle and King County, 1980.

Meinig, Donald W. *Continental America 1800–1867*. New Haven: Yale University Press, 1993.

———. "Isaac Stevens: Practical Geographer of the Pacific Northwest." *The Geographical Review* 45 (October 1955): 542–52.

Melina, Lois. "Politicos, Indians and the Press." In *Indians, Superintendents, and Councils: Northwest Indian Policy, 1850–1855*, edited by Clifford E. Trafzer. Lanham, Md.: University Press of America, 1986.

Miller, Daniel J., and Patricia R. Miller, with help from Jeanne Engerman and the staff of the Washington State Library. "What Did Chief Seattle Really Say?" Radio broadcast first aired on KKUP-FM, Cupertino, California, November 11, 1989. Duplicated typescript and bibliography obtained from Washington State Library, Olympia.

Miller, James E., Jr., ed. *Heritage of American Literature.* 2 vols. San Diego: Harcourt Brace, 1991.

Morgan, Murray. *Skid Road: An Informal Portrait of Seattle.* Revised ed. New York: Viking, 1960.

Murray, David. *Forked Tongues: Speech, Writing and Representation in North American Indian Texts.* Bloomington: Indiana University Press, 1991.

Murray, Mary. "The Little Green Lie." *Reader's Digest* 143 (July 1993): 100–104.

Nabakov, Peter, ed. *Native American Testimony: An Anthology of Indian and White Relations.* New York: Crowell, 1978.

Newspapers in Microform: 1981. Washington, D.C.: Library of Congress.

Nicandri, David L. "Isaac I. Stevens and the Expeditionary Artists of the Northern West." In *Encounters with a Distant Land: Exploration and the Great Northwest,* edited by Carlos A. Schwantes. Moscow, Id. : University of Idaho Press, 1994.

———. *Northwest Chiefs: Gustav Sohon's Views of the 1855 Stevens Treaty Councils.* Tacoma: Washington State Historical Society, 1986.

Perry, Ted. "Chief Seattle Speaks Again," *Middlebury College Magazine* 63, no. 1 (winter 1988/89): 28–30.

Prucha, Francis Paul, ed. *Documents of United States Indian Policy.* 2d ed. Lincoln: University of Nebraska Press, 1990.

Ramsey, Jarold. *Reading the Fire: Essays in the Traditional Indian Literatures of the Far West.* Lincoln: University of Nebraska Press, 1983.

———, ed. *Coyote Was Going There: Indian Literature of the Oregon Country.* Seattle: University of Washington Press, 1977.

Rich, John M. *Chief Seattle's Unanswered Challenge.* 1932. Reprint, Fairfield, Washington: Ye Galleon Press, 1970.

Richards, Kent D. *Isaac I. Stevens: Young Man in a Hurry.* 1979. Reprint, Pullman: Washington State University Press, 1993.

Ruby, Robert H., and John A. Brown. *A Guide to the Indian Tribes of the Pacific Northwest.* Norman: University of Oklahoma Press, 1986.

[Scammon, C. M.] "Old Seattle and His Tribe." *Overland Monthly* 4, no. 4 (April 1870): 297–302.

Seattle High School. *Sealth for 1904.* Seattle: Lowman and Hanford, 1904.

State of Washington, Indian Affairs Task Force. "Are You Listening Neighbor?" 1971. Revised edition, issued with "The People Speak, Will You Listen?" Olympia: State of Washington, 1978.

Stevens, Hazard. "The Ascent of Takhoma." *Atlantic Monthly* 38 (November 1876): 513–30.

———. *Life of Isaac I. Stevens.* 2 vols. Boston: Houghton Mifflin, 1900.

Stevens, Isaac I. Autograph letters to Mrs. Benjamin Hazard, August 28 and October 22, 1855. Beinecke Library, Yale University.

———. Letter to George W. Manypenny, December 26, 1853. In U.S. Senate, 33rd Congress, 1st sess., Executive Document 34 (1854): 6–9.

———. *Reports of Explorations and Surveys...for a Railroad from the Mississippi River to the Pacific Ocean.* Vol. 1. U.S. Senate. 33rd Congress, 2d sess., 1855; Vol. 12, parts 1 and 2. U.S. Congress. House. 36th Congress, 1st session, 1859. Executive Document 56.

Stevenson, Shanna. "The General Was a Dairy Farmer, Too." Olympia, Washington *Sunday Olympian,* "Totem Tidings" section (July 24, 1977), 12–13.

Swift, Jonathan. *Journal to Stella,* edited by Harold Williams. 2 vols. Oxford: Clarendon Press, 1948.

Thomas, Edward Harper. *Chinook: A History and Dictionary of the Northwest Coast Trade Jargon.* 2d ed. Portland: Binfords and Mort, 1970.

Trafzer, Clifford E., ed. *Indians, Superintendents, and Councils: Northwest Indian Policy, 1850–1855.* Lanham, Md.: University Press of America, 1986.

Warren, James R. *King County and Its Queen City: Seattle.* Sponsored by the Historical Society of Seattle and King County. Woodland Hills, Calif.: Windsor Publications, 1981.

Waterman, T. T. "The Paraphernalia of the Duwamish 'Spirit Canoe' Ceremony." Museum of the American Indian, Herge Foundation, *Indian Notes* 7 (1930): 129–48, 295–312, 535–61.

Watt, Roberta Frye. *Four Wagons West: The Story of Seattle.* Portland: Binfords and Mort, 1931.

Whitman, Walt. *Leaves of Grass.* Edited by Sculley Bradley and Harold W. Blodgett. Norton Critical Edition. New York: Norton, 1973.

INDEX